SPINNING FOR PIKE

Other Angling Books from David & Charles

R. C. R. BARDER

Spinning for Pike

WITH A FOREWORD BY
FRED. J. TAYLOR

DAVID & CHARLES

NEWTON ABBOT   LONDON   VANCOUVER

0 7153 6881 0

First published 1970 by Arco Publications
Second impression by David & Charles Ltd 1976

Printed in Great Britain
by A. Wheaton & Co., Exeter
for David & Charles (Publishers) Limited
Brunel House Newton Abbot Devon

For
Philippa, Edward and Charles

CONTENTS

ILLUSTRATIONS

FOREWORD

RICHARD WALKER, writing in *Still-Water Angling,* said: 'Alfred Jardine showed that it is possible to *understand* pike and how to catch them. Unfortunately he failed to pass on his knowledge through his writings.'

I believe this to be true. I believe that it *is possible* to understand pike and that this ability to do so comes only to those who are prepared to study, experiment and work hard on particular pike problems. I believe Dick Barder is such a person and that, unlike Alfred Jardine, he has passed on a wealth of knowledge in this book.

Like many anglers in this enlightened age Dick Barder does not like, nor see the necessity for, livebaiting, except perhaps in very special circumstances. He ends this book by suggesting that spinning is the most successful method of catching pike. Few anglers would agree with this at the outset, probably because they have not the ability to assess the various pike fishing situations with the degree of 'pike psychology' possessed by Dick Barder. They may think differently, however, after they have read it!

My own feeling is that the word 'successful' should be replaced by the word 'rewarding', for there is no doubt at all in my mind that spinning for pike can be made to work and can be *enjoyed* in all situations. Throughout this book the fact is made more and more obvious by the author.

Not everyone can be bothered to tackle the complex business of spinning for pike because of the difficulty in understanding the vast numbers of rigs, lures, tackles and methods involved, and yet I know from experience that there are many non-anglers who have taken it up on retirement and become successful. There are many others who would have done so if they could have read a down-to-earth book on how to go about it step by step. Now they will be able to do so, for, unlike many writers (myself included), Dick Barder does not make the mistake of assuming too much knowledge on the part of the reader: the details which the experienced angler/writer tends to skip over because he is sure that 'everyone knows that', are explained so that the non-angler can understand. That has obviously been the author's object from the beginning; to explain the complex business of spinning for pike so that it may be understood by anyone, be he novice or experienced angler.

I note that Dick Barder expresses his thanks to me for 'advice and encouragement in the preparation of this book'. I do not deserve these thanks. The book would still have been the excellent work it is without any help from me, but I am pleased to see some of my own ideas and tackle rigs described therein.

Pike spinning has been practiced for many years but it has never, to my knowledge, been the subject of a complete book: certainly the modern approach to pike spinning has not been so treated.

I have enjoyed many fishing days and days of argument and discussion with Dick Barder and I must confess to a feeling of deep satisfaction regarding my small association with this book. If I had to find any fault at all with it or the author, it would be to say that he is much too modest throughout.

FRED. J. TAYLOR

PREFACE TO THE FIRST EDITION

THE PAST twenty years have seen a quiet revolution in the techniques of freshwater fishing, and naturally enough many new books have appeared to cater for the ever increasing army of anglers.

It is not surprising that a number of these books deal with specialized methods of fishing and particular species of fish, but it *is* surprising that there do not appear to be any which are purely about spinning for pike, because spinning embraces a variety of successful techniques and is the favourite method of many anglers.

This book is an attempt to remedy this deficiency and to explain for newcomers to the sport the theory and practice of spinning for pike.

I wish to thank Fred. J. Taylor for all the advice and encouragement he has given me in the preparation of this book: my thanks are also due to the late D. A. R. Barder, Mrs B. R. Feldon, A. J. Forrester, A. Masterton-Smith, D. Morrel and Miss C. M. Walker.

PREFACE TO THE SECOND IMPRESSION

PIKE FISHING has increased enormously in popularity during the past few years and there are now many anglers whose greatest ambition is to catch a 20lb pike. This is a good thing because it means that more and more intelligent people will be trying to solve the problems of catching the big ones and will be sharing their knowledge with their brother anglers.

In this respect spinning as a method probably still offers most to the angler with an inquiring mind and I am confident that we shall hear of many more really big pike being caught on spun or worked baits in the future.

There is, however, one aspect of modern pike fishing that saddens me, namely the large numbers of keepnets that are used. Keepnets do more harm than good to pike and are only really necessary if a photo is to be taken or if you are taking part in a pike-fishing match. The rest of the time no useful purpose will be served by cooping up pike in a keepnet and I am sure the pike population would benefit if more fish were unhooked and returned to the water immediately.

Finally, I am glad to see that there are now so many artificial lures available at reasonable prices but I would warn the novice that some of these lures, particularly the plugs, only develop a really lifelike wriggling action if they are worked fairly fast. Others must be worked slowly or in jerks. Remember, it always pays to experiment.

R. C. R. BARDER

Ball Hill, Berkshire
1976

NOTE (see page 21) Since beaten by a 43 lb. pike caught by R. R. Whitehall in January 1974, using live bait, from a reservoir at Walthamstow. This fish has now been accepted as a new British and English record.

THE PIKE.

1. The Pike

THE SCIENTIFIC name for the pike is *Esox Lucius,* and it is generally called a pike be it large or small, but anglers have a number of colloquial names which denote its size. Thus a pike up to about two pounds in weight is a 'Johnny', while a fish between this weight and four or five pounds is a 'Jack'. It is rather unusual to hear a large pike referred to as a Jack but the term is equally correct, though obsolescent.*

The pike is the only member of its family found in the British Isles and is indigenous, but pike and a number of varieties occur widely on the North American Continent, in Europe, and parts of Asia.

---

* H. Cholmondley-Pennell's *Book of the Pike* is described by him on the title page as 'a Practical treatise on the various methods of Jack fishing'.

The pike has always captured the imagination of anglers and non-anglers alike—indeed it is one of the three particular sporting species instantly recognizable to the non-fishing public, the other two are the 'lordly' salmon and 'aristocratic' salmon-trout. This is rather unfair on the pike, who in terms of sheer size is comparable to the salmon, which only visits these shores to spawn, while the much vaunted salmon-trout exists purely for fishmongers and the ignorant, being in reality an ordinary sea-trout; another spawning-time-only visitor.

Once you have seen a pike you will neither forget it nor confuse it with any other fish. In my own case this dictum was impressed upon me at an early age, because I foolishly volunteered to remove the hooks from the jaws of a pike while its captor supposedly held them open. The jaws certainly opened very wide to admit my grubby hand but closed again with remarkable celerity; I carried the scars for nearly a year!

The best way I can describe this part of the pike's anatomy is to say that its jaw resembles the bill of a duck; spatulate and longer in the lower than the upper jaw. Line it with hundreds of hinged and backward pointing teeth, trim the lower edges with a smaller number of large teeth and you've got the idea.

The body is long and streamlined, the large rounded dorsal fin is set far back towards the tail which is slightly forked and also rounded.

The anal fin is positioned more or less under the dorsal fin and is a slightly smaller edition of it. The pectoral and pelvic fins are set to the rear of the gill covers and about half way along the belly respectively.

The colouration of the pike is as follows. Body pale green and covered with primrose, irregularly shaped and positioned spots, merging into a white belly and blackish brown back. The pelvic and pectoral fins are pinkish brown, but the tail, anal and dorsal are reddish brown with transverse and clearly defined bars of darker shades. All these colours may vary in tone depending on the locality of the pike and its condition. A pike from a shallow sand-bottomed stream will be paler than its cousin in a deep and sombre lake, and the colour scheme of a recently spawned pike will be altogether less vivid.

A slight difference will be noted in young pike, a stripey effect replaces the blotchy primrose spots. A young pike spends much of his time in the weedy margins of the water, where the stripes blend well into his surroundings, thus helping him in practice attacks on the young of the other fish; a further important function is to give protection against the assaults of older members of his own family. There's no tastier morsel for a big pike than one of his own descendants!

The eyes of the pike are large and are set towards the top of the flattened head, they are a cold greeny-yellow with blackish flecks, and are similar in size and colour to those of a leopard. I can personally vouch for this rather unlikely piece of information, because a taxidermist who mounted a pike for me tells me that the very realistic glass eyes he used were removed from the head of a similarly treated leopard!

A young pike. Note the striped markings. *Photo: Angling Photo Service.*

The skull of a large Irish pike that probably weighed more than 40 lbs. *Photo: G. Kinns.*

The pike is similar to the leopard in other ways, its spotted markings serving the same purpose, camouflage, but this is not so much a camouflage against potential enemies as a means of deceiving its intended prey; the pike, like the leopard, is entirely predatory.

Nothing that moves in or on the water is safe from the pike. He lives principally by devouring other fish but has also been known to attack and consume ducks, water rats, puppies and other small mammals. There are recorded instances of bathers, and horses which were drinking from the water being savaged.

I mentioned that the camouflage of the mature pike helps conceal him from his victim. This is an important point to remember because it provides an insight into his character. The pike is a lazy fish, and although there are occasions when he will actively course through the water in search of food, such as immediately after a period of enforced abstinence, he would infinitely prefer to conserve his energy by remaining motionless near the bottom, and wait for his victims to pass nearby.

The subsequent ambush is unbelievably quick and effective. The pike attacks with a rush, and seizes the helpless little roach, or whatever it may be, across the middle. Having crushed it between his powerful jaws he returns to his lair, to swallow it head first at his leisure.

It is obvious that upward-looking eyes are well suited to this mode of attack, but this is not their only advantage. The eyes of a pike can focus on an object ahead, rather as our own eyes can, whereas most freshwater fish have their eyes set too far to the sides of their heads. It is for this reason that a pike is able to look you straight in the face; but speaking for myself I would rather avoid the experience; the thought of a large pike lying on the bank and gazing reproachfully up at one is unnerving! But the pike does not rely entirely on his eyes to pinpoint likely victims, he is also extremely susceptible to vibrations in the water, indeed some modern authorities believe that the line of small holes which runs along the edge of a pike's lower jaw is a continuation of the lateral line, in which the sensory nerves of freshwater fish are concentrated, and his sense of smell is also well developed. Oddly enough it is rare for pike to feed in darkness, but they are obviously well equipped for muddy water conditions when visibility is poor.

The pike misses little of what goes on around him but these very weapons in his own armoury, his keen eyesight, sensitivity to vibration, strong sense of smell and predatory habits can all be turned against him by the skilful angler.

For convenience sake I have been referring to the pike as 'he'. The larger pike are in fact normally females. There are, of course, exceptions to this ruling, but you won't be far wrong if you assume that any fish over about 12 lbs. in weight is female, and even seasoned pike anglers have difficulty in deciding the sex of smaller fish.

From my own experience the figure and assumption are reasonably correct. I well remember that the first sizeable pike I caught in a little fished lake, which had enjoyed a reputation for monster fish in earlier days, was gnarled and thin looking. It was also blind in one eye, though none of these defects stopped it from putting up a quite remarkable resistance which left a permanent set in my rod. That fish weighed 14 lbs., and I concluded at the time that the fishery had deteriorated, and that 14 lbs. was about the best weight obtainable.

The subsequent capture of a number of larger fish, obviously in the prime of life, leads me to believe that the 14-pounder was in reality an old male, and I recall that it contained no spawn.

Its capture was effected by the use of a rather high herring, which was being slowly drawn through the water. Perhaps this crippled elderly fish was having difficulty in obtaining its food, in which case the herring must have appeared to be manna from heaven!

I find that I am already departing from the general to the particular, but the foregoing anecdote will serve to introduce a question of special interest to the pike man, namely its size.

The record Irish pike was caught in Lough Conn in July 1920 by John Garvin. Its weight was 53 lbs., the length 51 inches and girth 36 inches. A partially digested salmon nearly a yard long was removed from it before the weighing ceremony, otherwise it might have weighed some 60 lbs.!

It was caught by spinning a $2\frac{1}{2}$ inch copper and silver spoon. It is to my mind particularly significant that it took a spinner *after* eating a salmon, and I will discuss this point in a later chapter, but the fact that the Irish record was caught by a spinner at all is a useful weapon in an argument between the devotees of this and other methods; you are advised to note it well!

The record Scottish pike, which ranks as the British record[*], weighed 47 lb. 11 oz., and was caught in July 1945 by Thomas Morgan in Loch Lomond. Livebaiting was the effective method and the length was 53 inches. The girth, however, was but 19

[*] Since disallowed by the British Record Fish Committee on a technicality. But there is, in my opinion, no reason to dispute that this fish existed and was caught in the manner described.

A nice brace of pike. *Photo: Bill Keal.*

inches. I know few other details of this fish save that it was eventually cut up and distributed among six families for food, but I can't help wondering if it had recently spawned, which would account for that elegant waistline. The English record pike is no longer listed officially by the Record Fish Committee, which only concerns itself with British records. This is a pity, because pike are held in far greater esteem by the English than they are by either the Scots, Irish or Welsh, all of whom prefer the salmon; the fate of the British record is a mute testimony thereto. By some strange irony pike undoubtedly grow bigger in Ireland and Scotland than they do in England!

The English record is held by Mr P. Hancock. Caught in Horsey Mere in February 1967 it weighed 40 lbs.* Shortly afterwards a 39 lb. pike was captured by Mr C. Loveland in Knipton reservoir. The baits used were respectively worked deadbait,

*See page 14.

and a five pound pike livebait.

Both these fine sportsmen returned their fish to the water to live and fight again.

The keen student of pike lore has difficulty in getting used to the idea of these two monsters being caught within days of each other, because the previous record was a $37\frac{1}{2}$ lb. fish caught in the Avon by Mr Clifford Warwick as long ago as 1944, while the record prior to this had stood at 37 lbs. since 1879! I don't imagine that Alfred Jardine, the captor of the 1879 fish, thought for one moment that his record would stand for sixty-five years, but stand it did, though a Major Booth equalled it with a fish from the Wye caught on a spinner in 1910.

Alfred Jardine was a remarkable pike-fisherman. Not only did he hold the record but was also responsible for the downfall of a 36 lb. fish, a 31-pounder and at least sixteen others weighing more that 20 lbs.

In recent years I have fished a private lake that was almost certainly fished by Alfred Jardine and was definitely fished by Cholmondley-Pennell.

I went there once in the early morning. A mist covered the water, obscuring the ancient house and hiding the farther bank. I knew that soon the sun would rise, but for a little while I was alone.

Was it my imagination that something moved in the mist? Do the spirits of the Victorian pike masters revisit the waters they knew and loved so well?

I think they do; the pike I caught that morning were the descendants of the pike that they caught; perhaps, for a moment in time, a bond existed between us.

Now I referred earlier to the salmon removed from Garvin's pike before the weighing ceremony, and would add that 4 lbs. weight of fish was disgorged by Warwick's English record before it was weighed. One cannot help remarking on the casual attitude of these record holders. If I caught a record pike there would be no question of it opening its mouth to disgorge fish!

There is one further point to make about the captors of record pike, which is of interest. Without exception they are experienced anglers, with other monsters to their credit in several cases. This disproves the oft repeated theory that records are always broken by beginners, children, or old age pensioners!

There are a number of conclusions that can be drawn at this stage. The most obvious one is that a pike of say 35 lbs. could weigh 45 lbs. or even 50 lbs. if you were fortunate enough to catch it after it had swallowed a fifteen pounder, and there are several authentic cases of pike seizing and devouring fish weighing in excess of half their own weight. A second and unhappier conclusion is that a pike of 35 lbs. upped to a temporary 50 lbs. is unlikely to accept an angler's bait; but as I mentioned earlier, I shall have more to say on this subject.

The fish discussed so far are, of course, exceptional. A perusal of the angling journals over the last few years indicates that very few fish indeed weighing more than 30 lbs. will be caught in England during a season, but a dozen or so may be noted between 25 and 30 lbs. The number of fish recorded between 20 and 25 lbs. increases sharply, and 25 lbs. can be regarded as a reasonable optimum for most lakes, canals and rivers. The ideal conditions that produce the real monsters of 30 lbs. and more are rarely found.

Pike are normally accounted big at 18 lbs. and a 20-pounder was certainly worthy of a glass case in the days when taxidermy was fashionable.

Many authorities are of the opinion that bigger pike have existed than those caught by anglers, and a large number of fish are cited to make the point; some examples are the 170 lb. pike taken from a pool at Lillishall limeworks in 1765, the 52 lb. fish discovered when Whittlesea mere was drained in 1851, and the 60 lb. Cheltenham pike which was found dying of old age, blindness and starvation in 1896. Weighing in for the rod-caught fish is the famous Kenmure pike, the skull of which still exists, which weighed 72 lbs. and is believed to have

Horsey Mere, where the English record pike was caught. *Photo: Bill Keal.*

been caught by spinning.

Richard Walker, who is the man most responsible for the quiet revolution referred to in my preface, and who is noted for his accuracy and attention to detail in all matters piscatorial, believes in this fish, as did Cholmondley-Pennell who mentions it in *The Book of the Pike,* but it is probably best for you to form your own opinion on the whole fascinating subject of monsters whether legendary or otherwise, and a number of good accounts are given in two modern books, *The Fisherman's Bedside Book* by 'B.B.' and *Angling Ways* by Marshall Hardy.

If, when you have read these angling classics, you still have an appetite for mighty pike I refer you to my references, which are listed later, and the reading of as many books on the subject as you can lay your hands on will do much to engender a proper attitude to the serious business of catching big pike.

There is, however, another query which is often raised

concerning pike. Oddly enough the enquirer is usually not a fisherman, but the question, 'How old would a fish like that be?' is certainly of interest.

I myself am not scientifically trained, and only a scientist, or skilled scale reader, can accurately assess the age of any particular fish. One modern author reckons that a year per pound of weight gives a reasonable average indication, and the impressions I have gained from my own reading makes me think he is near enough, but the sort of conditions that produce monster pike might well speed up the process, while a poor water may produce ancient fish of very modest dimensions. The best advice I can offer, if you really must know the age of a fish you have caught, is that you should send a couple of dozen scales from the shoulder to a competent scale reader, and any fishing journal will tell you whom you should contact.

A pikey corner on Lough Ree. *Photo: Bill Keal.*

We have already established that the female pike is usually the larger and can now turn to a related subject, namely their love life.

In most waters pike spawn around the end of March, but inevitably seasonal and local variations of a month or even more, occur. One important factor is the weather, which should be mild, and the pattern of weather conditions in preceding months. A cold winter followed by a cold spring will delay spawning and vice-versa. Another factor is the actual state of the water. Pike, like insurance companies, are disturbed by storm, flood and tempest!

The place chosen for spawning will usually be a weedy sunlit shallow in a lake or canal, while river pike seek similar quarters by moving up into ditches or sidestreams.

The female pike may well be attended by a number of males, and the quantity of eggs laid will be enormous, several pounds of body weight in the case of a big one, but few of the eggs survive for long; they are a welcome meal for all sorts of fish, animals and birds living in, or near, the water.

Both male and female pike are exhausted by the fertilizing and egg laying processes, and it is generally agreed that some time must elapse before they are fit again, but whereas some authorities feel that it is early autumn before they are fully recovered, there are others who say that July is late enough.

It is probably fair to say that the recovery time will vary from place to place, fish to fish, and season to season.

2. Haunts and Habits

PIKE are widely distributed throughout the British Isles, and there are few waters containing fish that do not also contain a head of pike.

The purpose of this chapter is to discuss the haunts and habits of pike and the factors that influence them, but before doing so it would be as well to look briefly at their position in angling and piscine circles.

I am told that we live in a permissive age, but the old standards of conduct are still much to the fore in our attitudes to pike. Live and let live is no part of his treatment at the hands or boots of many anglers, who hasten his demise with smug satisfaction. 'After all they eat all the other fish, don't they?'.

The same people may sometimes be observed in winter bemoaning an apparent lack of pike; but that is by the way.

A more reasoned objection to his presence will be lodged by those with interests in rivers and lakes containing game fish. Such people, who are frequently not as wealthy as tradition would have you believe, are expecting to obtain some kind of return on an investment, a return which may be measured in terms of the pleasure derived from the fishing, and the subsequent eating of their catch, or even hard cash from the sale of fish or letting of rods. The knowledge that pike have appeared and are diminishing their assets is hardly calculated to please them!

The most ardent admirer of the pike must allow the justice of their actions in attempting to exterminate a very real menace, and can even profit thereby, with the oft added bonus of an invitation to come and try for trout in the summer if his efforts as a pest controller are successful.

Until fairly recently pike were tolerated in the majority of coarse fishing waters and were even introduced into a number of waters that did not formerly contain them.

The arguments put forward to establish the pike as a useful member of the community went something like this: the obvious reason why the roach (or whatever they may be) in such and such a lake or river do not reach a greater size is because there are too many of them competing for the food available. If we introduce some pike they will thin them out, and there will be fewer roach, which will be able to grow bigger. Bigger roach are more interesting to anglers than little ones, so the pike will be performing a useful service, as well as destroying weak or sickly fish that might otherwise spread disease.

An ingenious suggestion you will agree, but the course of events outlined will not necessarily occur. This is a shame, because even if the roach in question did not in fact grow any larger, at least their devotees would think they had, and would fish on in anticipation of every next fish being one of the missing specimens; both they and the pike men would be blissfully content.

The reasons why the introduction or encouragement of pike will not necessarily improve the quality of a coarse fishery are complex and beyond the scope of this book, but briefly (and there will be some exceptions) we can say that the factors that control the ultimate growth of the various species in any water are usually its size, and capacity to provide the right sort of living and feeding conditions. The introduction of pike will diminish the quantity of fish present, but will not affect these basic conditions which control their size. They will still grow only just as big as the potential of the water allows.

I can simplify the explanation by saying that the death of half a tribe of pygmies would not mean that the survivors would grow to normal stature in the foreseeable future.

It is now widely known that the summary introduction of pike into poorer waters will not always effect an improvement, and today's club secretaries employ a more scientific approach to the whole question of balanced stocking, whereas earlier generations tended to stock indiscriminately, finding rule of thumb cures for their difficulties. Their well-intentioned but uninformed activities may be partially responsible for some of the problems we now encounter.

Now you may think that no-one could possibly take exception to pike in larger, richer, waters with flourishing populations of all the coarse species, but this is not always the case. It has been suggested that there would be even more specimens among the smaller species if all pike caught were killed, instead of being returned to grow bigger as is normal practice, as more people prefer to fish for the smaller species than like to fish for pike. But in fact it is illegal to kill pike under certain specified size limits, and coarse fishermen as a race would be unlikely to adopt a course of action which might eventually deprive them of the choice of being able to fish for pike if they wanted to; apart from the moral and pike anglers' objections.

It would seem from the foregoing paragraphs that the only people who really like pike are pike anglers, and in general this is probably the case. Remember, however, that this has always been so. Thus Stoddart in the nineteenth century: 'But a pike, itself unpitying, unsparing, who would pity, who would spare?' While Ausonius expressed the fishes point of view as long ago as the fourth century: 'The wary Luce, midst wrack and rushes hid, the scourge and terror of the scaly brood'.

The opinions you form regarding the position of pike in society are of course your own affair, but they are unlikely to make much difference to the pike or anyone else, because in spite of all the movements for and against, in spite of the dreadful warnings given over the centuries that the quality of the pike fishing is deteriorating, or that the fish are doomed to extinction, the pike themselves continue to flourish, anglers continue to catch them, and the number of specimens of most species is on the increase.

It is high time I returned to the haunts and habits of pike. I will end this digression with the suggestion that you should not form set and inflexible opinions about the position of pike, but try to assess the situation in each different water you visit.

Now most books about pike fishing contain lists of likely pike haunts in lake or river, but no two lakes or rivers are identical, and conditions are constantly changing which precludes the possibility of such information having any more than a general application to the problem of pike location, unless the author explains, and his reader understands, why the pike chose such localities in the first place. The aspiring pike angler is advised to adopt a logical approach, based on a sound understanding of the known habits, character and preferences of his quarry and the factors that influence his movements; such knowledge, sensibly applied, will enable him to establish a working plan for finding pike in any type of water.

There are four main points to bear in mind when you look for a pike lie; the first three are concerned with the character and preferences of the pike, and the fourth will affect his habits and movements.

Pike are predatory, so the first qualification for a pike lie is that it should contain, be visited by, or be within striking

A 33 lb. pike caught by the author on a spinner.

distance of, quantities of smaller fish for the pike to feed on.
It will be unwise, subject to a number of other qualifications I
will outline shortly, to seek pike in places unattractive to the
food species—indeed Fred. J. Taylor of Aylesbury, the well
known author and angler, once remarked that the best way to
find a pike was to fish for roach, and although he was referring
to fishing in the Upper Great Ouse the thought is relevant;
ground bait attracts roach and they in turn may attract the
attention of a pike!

The second point concerns cover. We established earlier that
pike prefer to lie in ambush. Lakes, rivers, canals and ponds all
possess features in the shape of weedbeds, reeds, rushes, fallen
trees, deep holes, projections from the bank and projections in
and under the water which may provide concealment, and the
presence of one or more such features will be attractive to pike,
and very often to the food species as well. There is one exception to these thoughts about cover, which concerns really big

pike. These fish have so few natural enemies that they can afford to dispense with some of the concealment features sought by their smaller brethren.

I will call the third point the comfort factor. Pike are lazy fish with a marked preference for still or slowly moving water. This character trait is of little significance to lake anglers, but is very important indeed to river fishers, because the area of search can be narrowed down to those swims that are sheltered from the full force of the stream. It is interesting to note that such places often provide the necessary cover and are attractive to the food species as well; the faster the river the more the point applies; but don't forget that the pike themselves would prefer an easier existence and the bigger fish will drop downstream to quieter areas if they are able to do so.

All living creatures are affected by the seasons and the weather. Pike are no exception, so the fourth point is concerned with the time of year; the weather; and its effect on pike and their habits. Pike are cold blooded, which means that their metabolism will slow down in cold water and speed up in warmer water. Thus we can say that a cold spell may well put them off feed, though the pangs of hunger may eventually bring them back on feed if it continues for long enough, which may explain why it is sometimes possible to catch them in ice-fringed rivers and lakes. I think, however, that you should not attach too much importance to, or become unduly optimistic about this eventuality, because pike spend much less time feeding than digesting, and it is not unusual to see shoals of food fish swimming all round a pike, which will take not the slightest notice of them, while they in their turn seem able to sense that no danger exists—for the time being!

There are other occasions during the winter when every pike in a water appears to be on feed. It is not unreasonable to suppose that this event might follow a protracted spell of very bad weather, which may have frozen lakes and flooded or frozen rivers to such an extent that the pike were really starved, but a further possibility in this case is that a form of mass panic may

A 28¼ lb. pike caught by Fred. J. Taylor on a deadbait fished 'sink and draw'. *Photo: Bucks Advertiser.*

seize the shoals of food fish and their fear may be communicated to nearby pike who will also join the hunt and aggravate the situation still further; this might occur at any time of year.

The important point to remember about the weather is that a deteriorating situation decreases your chances, but improving weather has a good effect; a settled spell of warmer weather between cold spells can be very good indeed. Wind direction is only important in the way it affects the weather, and thus the water, but the effect of the weather on the feeding habits of pike is of considerable importance, as it will also affect their movements. In warm weather they may be found in any part of a lake or river that provides reasonable living conditions, as already outlined, but in cold weather both the pike and the fish they feed on will move into deeper, warmer water, and river pike may also be affected by floods, which will cause them to move into areas sheltered from the full force of the swollen river.

You should not imagine, however, that all pike in winter will always be found in the deepest and most sheltered areas of lakes and rivers, and three circumstances come to mind when they may once more seek shallow water. Firstly, it may have been cold for so long that all the water is equally chilled, secondly, the shallows may temporarily warm up in sunny and windless periods during a generally cold day, in which case some pike will be attracted to them by the warmth and will enjoy basking in the sun, while a third occasion is at the end of a cold winter, when the reproductive urge will tend to make them seek the shallower areas suitable for spawning.

I should mention in passing that pike are normally solitary fish. The only occasions when several are found together are just prior to and during the spawning period; when adverse conditions of cold or flood cause a number to share the same sheltered spot; and conversely, when conditions are so good that several will be attracted to the same area.

You may wonder at my interest in winter weather conditions and decide that the warmer more settled months are obviously better for pike fishing. Consider a moment.

The earliest day you may fish for pike is on June 16th, when the season which closed on March 14th re-opens, and in some areas the opening day for pike is later still. It is possible that you are an all-round fisherman, in which case you will probably prefer to fish for species such as carp, tench, or trout, because none of these may be fished for seriously in winter, either because they've hibernated or in the case of the trout because they're out of season.

If you are an absolutely dedicated pike-man you may avoid the water for other reasons. Firstly, you won't be popular with all the people fishing for other species and their number will be legion, secondly, the weed is going to hamper you, thirdly, you will be concerned with the physical condition of your favourite species, which may not have recovered from spawning. Come the end of September, however, the water will be yours. The weed will begin to die down and the pike become more active in search of food to build them up for the next spawning cycle; from October until Christmas they will be at their best. After Christmas they will start to fatten with spawn and the cold weather will slow them down—but this is the time when records are broken.

It is fair to assume that the majority of pike men will fish from October until March; my interest in the weather will be apparent.

I have outlined the four major factors that affect the location of pike and will now turn to their application.

There is an old military adage that time spent in reconnaissance is never wasted. I would suggest that your first visit to a new water will be well spent doing just this. It should include chats with local anglers, who seldom withhold information from serious enquirers; the garnering of as much information as possible about depths and subsurface features, careful examination of likely spots, and conjecture as to alternative areas that pike will move to if conditions change. Try also to see all the water; so many people fish at the nearest area to the access point. It is all too easy to dismiss a water as useless when a short walk around the circumference of a lake, or up and downstream in the case of a river, will reveal a variety of interesting and different possibilities.

Reconnaissance will produce all sorts of bits and pieces of

A pike, weighing 29 lb. 14 oz., caught by Bill Keal. But this one took bread-paste! *Photo: Bill Keal.*

information and indications of many places that may contain pike, but everything you learn should be matched to the four categories of preference and circumstance listed. It will be found, I think, that one or more of them will apply, particularly and obviously to those places that have a reputation for holding pike; but here lies a great danger.

You may have discovered a likely pike haunt and catch one or more pike from it. Alternatively, you may be told of such a place. As a result you make a beeline for it the moment you arrive at the water and are disagreeably surprised when you fail to catch a fish!

The normal reaction to this common situation is to place the blame on the fish for not feeding, or less usually on oneself for lacking the skill to catch them.

The possible truth of the matter is that your original assessment, or the recommendations you were given were excellent, but if you had thought to question your informant more closely he would probably have told you that he certainly caught pike in the indicated areas, but certainly not at this time of year, or never when it's this cold, or seldom when the current is really strong—the same sort of examination of your own original assessment, if you found the spot for yourself, may well reveal differences in conditions that caused the pike to move elsewhere. Thus it will be seen that excellent pike lies are excellent because pike frequent them more often than not for the sort of reasons that have already been explained, but equally if one or more of the factors that determined this state of affairs becomes really dominant the situation may change sufficiently for the pike to move elsewhere. Their new location will still fit within the four categories of preference listed, and may be only temporary, but it is up to the angler to decide which of the factors are most likely to affect the fish on the day he is actually fishing. They may well be obvious; floods and extreme cold are reasonable examples of the weather factor being dominant.

I suggest that the safest and surest way to avoid what I call the complacency trap is to reassess the situation each and every time you fish, along the lines I have stressed at such length; ignore for the time being opinions formed on other occasions and judge the desirability of the swim on its merits of the moment. If, having carried out this procedure, you are still unable to find the pike you will have been unlucky, but at least you will know that your failure was not due to any lack of enterprise on your part; success in pike fishing, as in many other spheres of activity, is closely related to the amount of intelligent effort devoted to it.

I will conclude this chapter by saying that you should now have good reason for thinking that river pike will often, but not always, be found at the edges of the main current in weirpools and millpools, near locks and lock cuttings, in the slacker water on the inside and outside of bends, in backwaters, in deep holes, downstream from projections from the bank, and in the water in the vicinity of islands, near the mouths of tributary streams and ditches, in holes under the bank, near weed beds and lily pads, in reed-fringed bays and weedy bays, below the piers of bridges, in deep and weedy stretches provided the current is not too powerful, in eddies and places where the general direction of flow is temporarily reversed, in all areas that provide good swims for the food species, and especially those food species that prefer gentler currents.

In all the places described where strong currents are adjacent to weaker flows, the pike, all things being equal, will frequently be found just nudging, but out of the main force of, the stronger current.

Pike in lakes are more difficult to locate due to the lack of current, but will often be found in deep holes, in reed-fringed bays, and remember that the pike like reed beds, off promontories, in or near weed beds and lily pads, in the vicinity of islands and other projections from the water, near the mouths of tributaries and ditches, where fences and the like run out into the water, near trees that have fallen into the water, near jetties and boat-houses, near the outflow if one exists, in areas frequented by the food species. The likely pike haunts I have listed for moving and still water are by no means a complete list, but they illustrate further the application of the preference factors. I repeat that none of these more obvious haunts should be taken for granted.

I think you will find, however, that the more you fish in all sorts of places the more you will develop the knack of pinpointing the best locations.

3. Other Methods

THIS is a book about spinning, but one good reason for describing livebaiting and deadbaiting first is to avoid confusion and further explanation later, while a second reason is that you will encounter a few waters and occasions when spinning will be ineffective, whereas another method, such as livebaiting or deadbaiting might possibly succeed.

It goes without saying that the angler, however dedicated to spinning, should not only be able to judge when and why the spinner will sometimes fail, but be ready, able and willing to change his tactics, because the prime purpose of pike fishing is to catch pike; the method should be the servant and not the master!

I do not intend to go into a great deal of detail about dead-baiting and livebaiting because in my opinion they are secondary methods, though I am not suggesting that they are ineffective as this is palpably not the case; but at this stage, and for the purposes of this book, I will limit my description of them to an outline of the principles that govern their use, and an explanation of how to recognize the places and moments when they will be better employed than the spinner. I will include the major variations of style in this chapter but I would prefer to leave the details of the tackle for the appropriate moment in another chapter.

Livebaiting then, which is an ancient and successful way of catching pike, is based firmly on the fact that pike eat other fish.

Many years ago it was realized that if one of the food fishes, such as a roach, rudd, bream, dace, chub, perch, gudgeon or even small pike could be armed with one or more hooks in such a way that it was still free to swim around, and if it was then allowed to roam in an area that the angler thought contained pike, there would be a good chance of it either finding a pike, or a pike finding it, with the result that the angler could hook the pike.

The only disadvantage of this plan is that the livebait is likely to conceal itself in the nearest natural cover without the angler realizing what has happened, so a large float is usually added, to keep it clear of the bottom, indicate its position, and signal the attentions of a pike. There are also two variations of style which differ from the simple livebait and float arrangement, these I shall describe in a moment.

Livebaiting has changed little since the days of Walton, but one change that has occurred is that it is no longer usual or even legal to allow the pike to swallow the livebait, which meant that all pike caught had to be killed, or if released were likely to suffer a slow death through having hooks in their intestines. Tackles used today are so designed that the angler may strike and set the hooks immediately the 'run' commences, with an excellent chance of hooking the pike firmly in its jaw and not in its throat or stomach.

The skilled livebaiter, who may fish from the bank or from a boat, will swing his livebait into all sorts of likely places, and will make it 'work' by applying pressure to the line in such a way that the bait will swim in the desired direction.

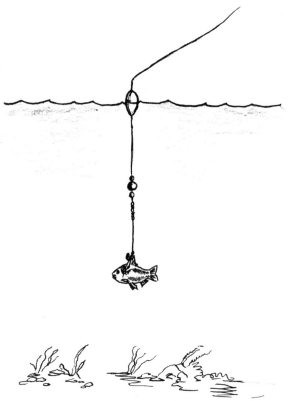

Fig. 1. Simple livebait rig.

An advantage which is often claimed for livebaiting, apart from the obvious one that the pike is being presented with a natural and genuine meal, is that it permits the use of a big bait, which small pike would have difficulty in seizing, and it is thought by many experienced pike anglers that a big pike, which feeds seldom, will be interested in a big bait, on the basis of the maximum return for the minimum effort.

Another advantage of the livebait is that it can be dropped into a small hole in a lily pad, weed bed, or other inaccessible spot at a distance from the bank,* where it would be difficult to use a spinner, and on these occasions the angler may well wish

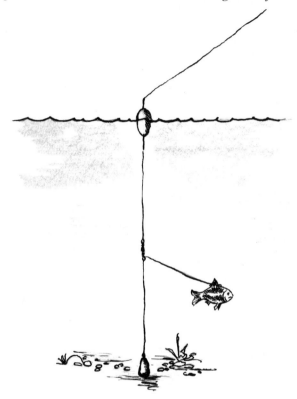

Fig. 2. Paternoster rig with float.

to limit the activities of his bait, which is where the paternoster and leger come into their own.

Paternostering consists of attaching a weight to the end of the line which is then wound taut between rod point and weight. The livebait is attached to the main line by a boom or

* There is an effective way of spinning in holes close to the bank, see Chapters 4, 5, 6 and 7.

link of line. Being tethered like a dog to a post, which in this case is the main line, it is free to move about, but only as far as the length of the boom or link permits. The particular advantage here, apart from the limitation of movement, is that the bait can be stopped from hiding itself or getting caught up in the bottom, if it should be weedy, by simply adjusting the distance from the anchor lead at which the link is affixed.

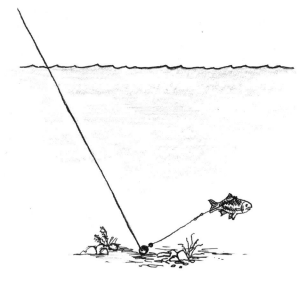

Fig. 3. Leger rig.

The leger achieves limitation of movement by the use of a running lead, which allows the line to pass through it as it lies on the bottom. A stop is fastened to the line on the baitward side and the line is wound taut, as in paternostering. The livebait is free to swim around in the area limited by the length of line between itself and the leger weight, but the particular advantage of the paternoster which I have just referred to is lost, though the likelihood of tangles is lessened.

Yet another occasion when livebaiting is useful is in very coloured water, such as occurs during floods or rainy conditions in many rivers and stream-fed lakes, or lakes which are exposed to high winds.

Pike are unlikely even to see a moving spinning bait in these conditions, unless it passes within inches of them and are often disinclined to feed anyway, but they can sometimes be persuaded to take a livebait.

We know that river pike prefer to avoid the full force of the current, and in flood time are very likély to hide up in lay-bys. The coloured water probably indicates the use of livebait and here again the leger and paternoster are effective, because the bait isn't swept downstream by the current. It is sometimes possible to judge the exact position of the pike, and it can be imagined that a precisely cast leger or paternoster can bring startling results.

Incidentally, there is nothing to stop the angler from adding a small float to his paternoster or leger to act as a 'tell tale'.

Deadbaiting, which accounts for a good number of large pike is by no means a new method, but it is one that had fallen into disuse, until fairly recently.

It owes its present popularity to a number of articles that appeared about it in the angling press, which were written by Fred. J. Taylor of Aylesbury, who, with his brothers, was largely responsible for its development into a practical means of pike-catching.

The Taylor brothers noted that pike could be caught by fishing for them with a dead fish, which was allowed to lie on the bottom of a lake. At first they thought that this was because they were fishing a water where livebaiting was a popular style, and they reasoned that the pike had become used to retrieving dead and discarded livebaits that had sunk to the bottom. Experiences on other waters where livebaiting was not the custom convinced them that the deadbait was effective in its own right; though whether the pike were scooping up the deadbaits because they represented an easy meal or because of a scavenging instinct is not quite certain; what was certain was that they and other anglers caught some very large pike!

. It was particularly remarked that deadbaiting was not so successful on warm bright days in winter as it was on overcast days, but in conditions of extreme cold it was more effective than either spinning or livebaiting. Fred. J. Taylor attributes the success of deadbaiting in very cold water to the fact that pike are unwilling to move very fast to follow a spinner, or capture a gyrating livebait, but are prepared to move slowly, and in their own good time as it were, to a dead fish laid on the bottom. The most popular deadbait is probably the herring which will defeat the attentions of baby pike as well as emitting a fishy, pike-attracting smell, but any of the food fish will serve.

Deadbaiting can be used in rivers as well as in still waters, but its use is limited in either to clear and weed free areas.

I am not by nature a person who enjoys deadbaiting because I only need five minutes to convince myself that the bait is firmly concealed in a weed bed, but deadbaiting is linked in my mind with spinning for rather unusual reasons.

I had been fishing for pike with moderate but not outstanding success for some years.

One day I called at the well-known aquarists and fishing-tackle shop in the Vauxhall Bridge Road. I selected a number of spinners and passed the time of day with the assistant, whose name I recollect was Owen.

Mr Owen, like most people in the tackle trade, is an angler himself and he enquired whether I had had any success with the pike that season. It so happened that I'd had a good day's spinning the previous weekend and naturally enough I was delighted to tell him about it.

Mr Owen listened politely. 'How about you?' I asked.

I listened enthralled as he told me about the pike, $32\frac{1}{2}$ lbs. no less, that he'd recently caught; it had run eighty yards after picking up his herring in a Middlesex gravel pit, and delving in his pocket he produced a photograph of himself and the monster fish, which ultimately ranked as one of the biggest of the season.

Bill Keal and another big pike weighing 29 lb. 12 oz. *Photo: Bill Keal.*

There and then I decided that I too would catch an enormous pike; from that moment on pike fishing became an obsession.

Eventually, fishing the shallows of a lake from a rubber dinghy, I realized my ambition.

By a strange quirk of fate the advice, never to neglect the shallows, was given to me by Fred. J. Taylor, the master deadbaiter. But I caught my fish on a spinner!

I believe that Fred Taylor was as pleased about it as I was.

4. Spinning for Pike

THE DICTIONARY defines spinning as fishing with a revolving bait, but most anglers will agree that there are a number of other styles which can broadly be classed as spinning, in which the bait does not revolve.

The same principle, however, applies to all of them; the bait must be cast out and drawn back through the water, but in such a way that a pike will be lured into seizing it, and unless the bait is given movement and a semblance of life through the agency of the angler himself it will cease to be really effective.

Spinning, then, is an active sport, but there is added enjoyment and even artistry in its skilful execution. Every cast calls for perfect co-ordination between hand, eye and mind; every retrieve is a test of the angler's ability to work his bait with intelligence and imagination. Anticipation too, surely one of

49

A 20-lb. plus pike taken on a spinner by Bill Howes. *Photo: Angling Photo Service.*

angling's greatest pleasures, is ever present. Any moment the rod may buck to the savage tug of a taking fish—a fish, more-over, that might be three feet long, with jaws like a crocodile, that will fight like a demon for fifteen minutes, twenty, perhaps even longer, until finally, sullenly, it comes to the net.

The purpose of this chapter, however, is not to enlarge on the joys of spinning, which I hope you will discover for yourself, but to talk a little about its philosophy.

Now, I have already outlined the principles of spinning, but the baits and the reasons pike take them, the methods and the reasons for using them, are of paramount importance.

There are two types of spinning bait. Natural and artificial. Natural baits are usually dead food fish and they can be wobbled, spun or fished sink and draw. The object in every case is to give the bait movement and life, but newcomers to pike fishing, and even older hands, may think it curious and unlikely to be successful compared with a naturally presented live or deadbait.

Why, after all, should a pike follow and seize the one fish in the vicinity that behaves in a suspicious, unnatural fashion?

We shall never know for certain until we find a talking pike, but it is logical to presume that a pike will take a spinning bait for the very good reason that it *is* behaving strangely, and is thus considerably more interesting and conspicuous than a fish behaving naturally.

Look at it from the pike's point of view. First of all his early warning radar system picks up an unusual vibration. It's obviously nothing to do with that shoal of roach over there, which he's ignoring, because he had a good feed yesterday, and which, dare I say it, might conceivably contain a perfectly presented livebait! Suddenly he sees the cause of the disturbance. All his senses are alert now. It's a fish all right but there is obviously something wrong with it, because it's lurching and falling through the water and suddenly it climbs towards the surface. All very odd; perhaps it's wounded?

Good heavens, here it is again—only it's closer this time and is swimming even more irregularly. The temptation and the curiosity it arouses are too much for master pike. Like a submarine going to action stations he is after it and the spinner claims another victim!

There is a very real difference between the philosophies of live and dead baiting and spinning.

In the first two methods the angler relies on placing an absolutely natural food item in an absolutely natural manner, as close as possible to a pike, or where he thinks there is a pike. He then sits back and awaits events; if there isn't a feeding pike in the place he selects he's out of luck.

The spinner, however, does not await events, he creates them, by taking the initiative from the start. The pike may be feeding well; in which case he covers plenty of ground, or rather water, and catches several fish. But if the pike are not feeding so well he covers even more water; frequently changing his lure, methods and tactics. Sooner or later, depending on his knowledge and experience, he will find a pike that can be enticed into seizing his bait. There are few days when the spinner is fishless.

Please do not think, however, that in averring the general superiority of spinning as a style of catching pike I am in any way denigrating the alternative styles of dead and livebaiting. This is certainly not my intention. They both catch fish and if an angler enjoys them more than spinning then that is entirely his own affair. The solace we gain from angling is personal to the individual concerned, it has absolutely nothing to do with anyone else.

Artificial baits are man-made, but there are two reasons why many of them were not particularly successful in their early days.

One reason for their lack of success was that spinning tackle, particularly in the case of reels and lines, was inefficient compared with modern tackle.

It was difficult to cast any small natural or artificial bait a reasonable distance unless considerable weight was added to overcome the inertia of the reel and the considerable friction of the heavier lines, then used, if the bait was cast from a coil of line.

Using a heavy bait or adding weight to it or the trace appeared to solve the problem, but in fact it did not, because a weighted lure sank very fast and constantly fouled the bottom unless it was retrieved even faster. Pike are lazy fish and the fast moving spinner was only of interest to the smaller, more active pike.

Now this sort of difficulty can hardly have helped, but it does explain perhaps why the majority of pike anglers then, and a number of anglers now, were and are convinced that spinning only catches small pike, and it also explains why Victorian and Edwardian anglers approved of trolling, which is the correct name for fishing sink and draw, because trolling, when practised with a long rod and natural baits in deep holes near the banks of lakes and rivers, does not involve long casts and extra weights. The bait can be allowed to sink and then be 'drawn' at a reasonably slow and big pike-attracting rate. Trolling is an effective method and I was referring to it in the last chapter when I mentioned a spinning technique that could be used in deep holes close to the banks of weedy waters.

The second reason why many early artificials were unsuccessful was that their design was based on the wrong principles.

I think it would be true to say that many anglers in the past, and indeed a number of present-day anglers, thought or think that an artificial should be the best imitation possible of a natural bait, and this is probably why so many of them were made to resemble small fish; but an exact imitation of a natural bait in metal, or what you will, is likely to be easily detected as a fake when worked slowly enough to interest a big pike—in much the same way that a painstaking copy of a well-known picture by a famous artist will not stand the scrutiny of an art expert.

Here, I believe, we have the fundamental reason for the failure of so many of the early artificials, but the majority of their designers and users not only failed to understand that an artificial bait should simulate the life and movement of a skilfully worked deadbait, rather than merely imitate its appearance: they also failed to realize that it should be a lure, relying as much, or even more, for its success on arousing the instincts of its quarry, as on giving the impression of being some kind of food fish—just, in fact, as a picture that gives the impression that it is an unknown work by a famous artist will always interest and sometimes deceive the art experts.

It is interesting to note that the same thinking applies to the lure flies used by loch and reservoir fishermen for trout. They bear little or no resemblance to food items when they are still, but once they are imbued with life and movement by the angler they take on the same sort of nebulous, intriguing quality that is possessed by good artificial pike lures, and I do not think there is much doubt that if trout fishing custom allowed a vibratory element to be included in their make-up, which is another feature of many modern artificials used for pike fishing, they would be even more effective.

There are many different types of artificial lure available today, which may flash, wobble, vibrate or revolve, indeed some of them perform all these pike-attracting activities simultaneously. I don't think it is unreasonable to suggest that fishing with them can even be an improvement on fishing with natural baits, because man's ingenuity can be applied to the design of the lures themselves, as well as to the methods of working them.

I have no doubt that many of the expert anglers who believe in spinning with natural baits will greet this suggestion with amazement, but having stuck my neck out this far I might as well take a further step towards the block; small baits, in my opinion, are more likely to catch large pike than big ones.

Let me deal with this last point first. It is well known that large hungry pike prefer to eat big fish, hence the big fish, big bait theory, and the great advantage claimed for livebaiting and static deadbaiting is, of course, that they allow the use of big baits. We mustn't forget, however, that large pike only feed hard and hungrily at long and irregular intervals.

As I see it this means that even if an angler is clever or lucky enough to place his live or dead bait in the right place, the odds are still against it being there at the right time, and there is no guarantee either that a wary old pike will take it in preference to all the other food fish available.

Now you may suggest that a big bait would probably be taken if it was presented to the pike in a more intriguing manner. Why not try spinning a big deadbait over it?

Well, I agree that a spun or worked deadbait would stand a greater chance of success than a naturally presented livebait or a static deadbait, and this I believe is why so many experienced anglers prefer to spin with big natural baits.

But let me dwell enviously for a moment on the circumstances surrounding the capture of the record Irish pike.

It fell, you will recall, for a small artificial lure. Now we know it wasn't at all hungry, because it had already devoured a sizeable salmon. For this reason I cannot believe it would have

Fred. J. Taylor's reserve supply of pike lures. *Photo: F. J. Taylor.*

been interested in a big spun or worked deadbait, nor, for that matter, a big livebait or static deadbait, but it might well have been interested in a skilfully worked small deadbait, had one been offered to it—and that, of course, is just what tempted the English record pike.

I am not suggesting you see, that big baits don't catch big pike, of course they do, sometimes, but I do think that a smaller bait stands a better chance on most of the occasions we fish, and if we work it slowly enough to tempt a lazy big 'un, why, he'll take it if he's hungry too!

I will now return to my first contentious suggestion.

Suppose, that instead of offering a large pike a pleasant little snack during one of those long and frequent periods when he isn't interested in a big meal, you asked him to try a fabulous new cocktail—one he had never heard of before. Don't you think he would want to taste it, even if he had just eaten?

I think he would.

To my mind it is in just this sense that good artificials are often superior to small spun natural baits.

Ah well, it is probably impossible to be absolutely right or completely wrong about anything in angling, but I shall still have succeeded in my task if I've lured you into thinking about it all, and it's the anglers who think who catch the fish!

5. Spinning Rods, Tackle and Baits

THE MAJORITY of modern anglers who spin for pike use mass-produced fixed spool reels, short lightweight rods and nylon lines, which enable them to cast light baits accurately and far with the minimum of practice and dexterity, but only a few decades ago it was customary to use much heavier rods, anything up to, or even more than twelve feet in length, silk lines 'strong enough to hold a fish of forty or fifty pounds', and centre pin reels. It is not surprising that considerable manual dexterity was needed to use such an outfit successfully.

There are, inevitably, a number of people who decry the use of modern tackle on the grounds that it reduces spinning to a boring mechanical exercise totally lacking in skill and artistry, but I suspect that their judgement is clouded by sentiment; I cannot see why spinning with modern gear should be a boring mechanical exercise unless the angler himself is a dull and unimaginative fellow; if this is the case the same thought can also be applied to spinning with old fashioned tackle; you need only substitute 'manual' for 'mechanical'. Likewise skill and artistry are not concerned with the equipment we use, but with the way we use it.

The purpose of the rod, reel and tackle in spinning is the same as it has always been, to help the angler cast and retrieve his bait and play his fish, but modern equipment has benefited from the scientific advances of the twentieth century; its use makes it easier and quicker for the individual to acquire skill as an angler because it assists him in overcoming the basic problems of manipulating his tackle and replaces to a certain extent the manual dexterity that was needed to use old-fashioned gear. In much the same way it is easier and more practical to learn to drive and use a modern automatic car than a veteran: but the man behind the wheel of a modern car is not necessarily a good driver; whether you succeed as a pike fisherman will depend in the final analysis on you yourself, not your equipment!

The criticisms that are levelled at modern equipment, however, do not stop short at artistry and skill. It is also suggested that long rods are better instruments for striking and playing a pike, because they give greater control and act as better shock absorbers, while centre pin reels are more sensitive due to the absence of gears between angler and fish. It is true, of course, that long rods perform better when it comes to playing a fish, but there is no doubt that short rods and fixed spool reels are a more practical proposition for casting light baits. What it all boils down to is that old-fashioned rods and centre pin reels were good for striking and playing, but bad for casting light baits, whereas short rods and fixed spool reels are good for casting both light and heavy baits, but bad for hooking and playing the pike.

But is it really necessary to follow an old tradition, or accept a modern extreme, when neither is capable of doing more than half the job efficiently? I think not. Modern tackle, however, has many variations which allow us to make an effective compromise. This, surely is its real advantage, so I will now assume that you, like me, would actually prefer to use an outfit that combines the facility of being able to cast both light and heavy baits with the ability to hook and control a large pike effectively; the recommendations I shall make are based on this assumption.

Now rods, reels and lines are obviously interdependent and should be matched to each other, but I think that I should treat them individually at first to establish the qualities we are looking for in each, and conclude my remarks with suggestions for what I hope you will agree is a suitable 'marriage'.

Choosing a suitable outfit for spinning is, in fact, not dissimilar to falling in love and getting married, with the advantage, if advantage it is, that you can still go out with all your old girl friends and practice polygamy as well; but women and fishing tackle can both be expensive, and if I had had more experience and knowledge ten years ago I should have saved myself a great deal of trouble and money. My own experiences may well be of interest, because they represent the efforts of an ordinary angler to obtain a suitable outfit. I hasten to add, however, that I am referring only to fishing tackle and will continue to do so!

I started my pike fishing career shortly after the war, with a four foot bait-casting rod and multiplier reel that my father had brought back from a visit to America. Rod and reel were perfectly matched for casting provided the bait wasn't ultra-light, and the outfit was much admired, but I often wonder what would have happened if I had hooked a really heavy fish. Other outfits followed, but eventually, when pike fishing became my favourite sport and spinning my favourite method I became dissatisfied with my growing collection of tackle that wasn't absolutely right and decided I would obtain a really super outfit. But before I tell you about it, I had better say that I don't intend to continue indefinitely to talk about fixed spool or multiplier reels without explaining the principles of their construction and use. Their turn will come; at the moment you will not be misunderstanding me if you don't know what they are.

To return to my outfit. My first object was to find a rod that possessed the desirable casting and fish playing qualities referred to earlier. I knew by now from my reading and observation that I needed a powerful rod, with a progressive action right through to the butt to play the heavy fish I hoped to catch, but it had to be sensitive enough to cast a light artificial lure. I knew too that I could test the power of a rod by tying one end of a piece of string to the rod point and the other to a spring balance—by pulling the rod round until its tip was at right angles to the butt I should obtain a reading. A suitable rod would have a test curve of between $1\frac{1}{2}$ and 2 lbs. At the same time I would check to see if the rod bent into a semi-circle, because if only the tip pulled round the rod would be bad for casting all but the lightest baits and would straighten itself too quickly when flexed. This sets up a nasty jagging action that can jerk out the hooks when playing a fish, instead of acting as a strong but supple shock absorber.

I had also learnt that a rod that 'springs' from immediately in front of the butt, when it is jerked sharply from side to side, would be a better caster than one that had either a floppy action in the middle of its length or a purely tip action.

I had considered at length the material from which it would be made. Split-cane is sensitive and fairly light. Each individual fibre fights back more strongly the more the rod is bent, but split-cane can be disappointing unless it is perfectly tempered, and it is impossible to tell the difference between good and bad cane without being an expert. I considered briefly solid fibre glass, a cheaper material, but it is heavy in the right sort of length, though the action can be sweet in a short rod, as I knew already from using one. Should I perhaps try the controversial hollow fibre glass rods? Fibre glass is very light and almost unbreakable, but its power decreases as the curve in the rod increases and the tube flattens, giving a soft action compared with the steely action of cane. Then too there are steel rods, which many people speak well of, but something in me recoiled from the thought, though one day I certainly intend to try one.

Then, of course, there's length to be considered. The shorter the better for comfort and lightness, not to mention precise one-handed casting with either fixed spool or multiplier, but what about control and the power to strike the hooks hard into the jaw of the pike, which might be thirty yards or more away? Opinions seemed to vary between seven and ten feet. Even a ten-foot rod would weigh but a fraction of the weight of earlier rods, if made in hollow fibre glass, and a long rod is useful if the banks are boggy or lined with reeds.

But what about fittings? Did I want a long handle with a sliding, locking reel grip so that the reel could be moved up or down depending on whether I wanted to cast single-handed or double-handed? Or did I want a fixed reel position which would limit me to choosing between the two styles? Double-handed casting is fine for distance with a long rod, but single handed rods are more delicately accurate. In any event the fish must be played single-handed, because one's other hand would be on the reel handle. Then too there are rod rings to be remembered, these must be made from some really hard substance or grooves will appear and fray the line. Their size and quantity is also important.

Eventually I visited two or three tackle shops. Unfortunately, I had chosen a time when stocks were low, and although I quite liked several rods I didn't see exactly what I was looking for.

Then I had an idea. People who spin for salmon need rods with many of the qualities of pike-spinning rods. I went to a firm that specialized in game fishing tackle. They were able to show me a number of rods which were designed for light or heavy salmon spinning; there were single handed rods up to about eight feet and double-handed rods up to ten feet or so in length, made in both cane and hollow glass. I settled for a $7\frac{1}{2}$ foot split-cane model with a test curve of about $1\frac{1}{2}$ lbs. It's a joy to use, but I soon realized that it was a little too short, and although the action is excellent it lacks real stopping power and the ability to control heavy fish. My next move was to make an eight foot split-cane rod that could be used single or double-handed with a fixed spool or multiplier reel. I am no rod maker, but there are excellent kits available. The one I chose was modified slightly to try and give exactly the sort of action I wanted. Unfortunately the rod ended up with too much tip action for my liking, but a friend of mine was very taken with it and purchased it from me. I regret that rod now, it has been instrumental in landing a number of specimen pike and a salmon of fifteen pounds!

I have now made another 8-foot rod in hollow fibre glass. The reel fittings slide on the long cork handle to allow for double or single-handed use, but I intend to modify it to being a purely single-handed rod. It is immensely powerful, and the length, for me at least, is just right. It will cast a light or even very heavy bait with ease, and the test curve is in the region of two pounds.

Why did I change to hollow fibre glass? My little split-cane rod is no longer perfectly straight, because I used it once to cast a heavy deadbait and overloaded it. Hollow fibre glass will stand any amount of overloading without damage. It is, therefore, more versatile. Incidentally, the action of hollow fibre glass rods is constantly improving as new techniques of manufacture are developed. I think that in a few years time it will equal that of split cane.

Choosing a rod that really suits you and is suitable for the job is tricky, and I shall have more to say about rods in a moment, but the reel too is important and must work well with it.

A spinning reel must release line easily so that a light or heavy bait can be cast by the rod. It must also retrieve line and enable the angler to keep in touch with the fish.

The fixed spool reel was invented in 1905 by a Mr Illingworth. It works on the principle that it is easier to pull line off the end of a spool than to have to make the spool revolve. You can check this by turning a cotton reel so that the hole that the

Fixed-spool reel: casting position.

Fixed-spool reel: playing a fish. The finger is applied to the spool to give extra braking power.

spindle runs through is towards you, and pulling off the cotton. Try again with the spool at right angles to you, using a match as an axle. The difference is considerable. But once the line is off the spool it must be easy to put it back on, or retrieve it. The obvious solution is to have some means of turning the spool at right angles with the rod again, but line gets a twist in it through being pulled off the end of a spool, this is not removed and can be troublesome if this solution is adopted, so a pick-up is used that lifts out of the way before the cast and clicks back to retrieve. The pick-up is mounted on the 'flier' which travels round and round the spool as you turn the reel handle and winds the line back onto the spool, dekinking it the while; additionally the spool moves forward and back to ensure the line winds on evenly.

What happens when you hook a big fish that takes line fast? It's no use opening the pick-up, the fish would be running around with no pressure being exerted. In fact the spool, which is mounted on an axle, is free to turn and give line against an adjustable brake or slipping clutch. The angler can reinforce its action, or even stop it giving line completely, by placing his forefinger on the rim of the spool. He doesn't touch the winding handle however, because winding against a running fish would not be a positive control and would kink the line again.

Fixed spool reels are used for every sort of freshwater fishing except flyfishing and many sorts of sea fishing these days, but no-one wanted to know about them in 1905 or for many years afterwards. The reason for this is that fine lines were needed, that slipped easily over the rim of the spool. Fine lines in those days had a low breaking strain and the majority of anglers did not understand how to use the slipping clutch to control a running fish. Today we have nylon monofilament lines that have a smooth surface and a natural springiness that suits them admirably for use with fixed spool reels. They are immensely strong for their diameter, compared with earlier types of line, and many monster fish of all species are caught every season by anglers using these lines and fixed spool reels.

The start of a typical cast using a fixed-spool reel.

The critics of fixed spool reels today base their criticisms on the insensitivity of the reel when line is retrieved or a fish played because there can be a lot of gearing which is necessary, of course, to overcome the difficulties that occur when the drum of a reel is parallel, instead of being at right angles to the rod, but not all fixed spools suffer from an excess of gearing, and it is a small price to pay when the many advantages and tremendous versatility of the reel are considered.

I will now list some points to look for when you choose a fixed spool reel. Choose a well-known make, and buy an expensive, rather than a cheaper model. It is likely to run more smoothly and have greater durability. See that it can be shaken hard with the pick-up, or bale arm as it is also known, in the open position. If it releases itself without the winding handle being pushed firmly forward, which is how the release is normally effected to start the retrieve, it won't be very good for spinning. One day when you make a really vigorous cast it will release itself as you cast. The progress of your spinner will be sharply arrested and it will lash back round your ears and face. Ask about the line capacity of the reel. The spool must take at least one hundred yards of nine or ten pound nylon line. Check at the same time that the adjustable drag, which may be on the front of the spool, on the winding handle, or, depending on the make, at the rear of the reel, is sensitive and does not lock the spool abruptly as you tighten the knob. Look carefully at the bale arm. Is there a rotating roller bearing where the line curves sharply round it when you retrieve? It's better for the line and gives greater sensitivity if there is no resistance at this point, but it is not strictly necessary and some good quality reels do not possess this feature.

The winding handle is important too. Some reels have handles which can be attached to either side of the body to give left or right hand wind, they may also fold for ease of packing. Reel handles must lock firmly in the working position. There is nothing more irritating than a handle that decides to fold itself away, or even detach itself from the reel as you play a big fish!

Ask too about the gearing of the reel. It is unnecessary to have several gears between the reel handle and the rotating pick-up, ideally there should be a direct drive between them. Most fixed spool reels have an anti-reverse device. If there wasn't one and a big fish made a sudden run against a heavy brake setting the reel would give line by turning backwards, but a winding handle that is turning backwards fast is difficult to control! It is customary to play the fish with this check in the 'on' position, but it should be switched off at the moment of landing the fish in case it makes a sudden last plunge, a backward spinning handle, then, is better than a broken line. Lines can be easily broken when the rod is held upright and doesn't give so much shock-absorbing effect and the fish is on a short line. One make of reel has three positions for the anti-reverse control, 'on', 'off', and 'off' against a light check if the handle should run backwards. The same model also has a spool that travels forward at one speed and back at another so that the line can never bed into itself; it leaves the spool very easily indeed during the cast.

You should check the speed of the retrieve. A very fast retrieve is not a good feature in pike spinning reels because it encourages you to retrieve the bait too fast. Most of the better makers produce models with differing speeds. You can safely choose one with a slower rather than a faster rate. I think it is also worth considering a closed face reel. These work on the same principle as a fixed spool reel, but the spool is not visible. It is not possible to brake the spool with the forefinger but the best of them have really sensitive and positive mechanical brakes. I suspect that these reels will eventually supersede the standard fixed spools, and they are already much used for spinning on the Continent.

Multiplier reels were first in use long ago. They work on the principle, when used as casting reels, that a very light spindle is more easily turned than a heavy drum. The axle of the spindle which holds the line is, of course, at right angles to the length of the rod and gears are fitted so that the line can be retrieved quickly enough onto the very small diameter lightweight spool; hence the name multiplier. Good multipliers have a release device which lets the spool disengage from the gears and handle during the cast, allowing it to run very freely. One of the problems that used to be encountered with multipliers was backlash. The spool would still be spinning very fast as the bait hit the water. The angler controlled the running of the spool by delicately applying his thumb to it. With practice, backlash and overruns could be avoided, but modern multipliers do the job for you, by monitoring the speed of the spool with centrifugally operated brakes. The best multipliers I have seen are Swedish, the one I use never suffer from overruns at all as long as I keep my thumb away from the spool! Most good multipliers have a 'traveller' that runs backwards and forwards in front of the spool to wind the line evenly, a control to set the braking devices for your weight of bait, and a ratchet brake. The fish is controlled when hooked by thumb pressure on the spool, often in conjunction with an adjustable drag brake incorporated in the winding handle.

Multipliers are better for playing heavy fish than fixed spool reels, you can also cast a heavier bait further with a multiplier because the spool, once running, does not offer the resistance of its own inertia, and gets lighter as more line leaves it. Conversely the weight of the projectile, i.e. bait and line, increases as the cast progresses and the bait travels farther away. On a fixed spool reel the lip of the spool offers more and more resistance as the quantity of line on the spool diminishes during the cast. Hence my remarks about large line capacity spools which delay this effect. Fixed spools, however, cast light baits better than multipliers, and it is easier to cast into all sorts of holes and corners, because no jerk is necessary to overcome the inertia of a spool and start it revolving.

Once again it pays to buy the best if you decide to buy a multiplier, but the choice in England is limited. Possibly the best which are readily obtainable are the Swedish A.B.U.s but there may well be comparable British and American models

The start of an overhead cast using a multiplier reel.

that have escaped my notice. In any event the multiplier of your choice should hold at least one hundred yards of 10 lb. line, and have an ultra-light spool to give you the best chance possible of casting light lures without having to add extra weight. The braking, spool release, and level wind features are obviously desirable, and the reel should take apart easily for cleaning and oiling.

I now come to centre pin reels. It is possible, if you are the sort of person who plays tennis for his county, or are a lineal descendant of Alfred Jardine, that you will master the cast from a centre pin reel. But even if you are in this category you will still need weight, and room around you to cast. There are moments, of course, when you will want weight, such as when fishing a powerful river in order to keep the bait down, and there are other times when weight is already with you, such as when you use a heavy natural bait. On these occasions you can use a centre pin to advantage, and if you hook a good fish you will be able to play and control it without a gearbox between you. Most people, however, avoid spinning with centre pins because of the difficulty of casting without overruns and the limitations imposed on the weight of bait that can be used; by fishing with a fixed spool reel or even a multiplier they can do everything that can be done with a centre pin, and a great many more things besides. If you do decide to try spinning with a centre pin, however, you have my respect and admiration. You should look for a reel that is light, well-balanced and extremely free running. It should have an adjustable drag brake to help overcome overruns, a ratchet brake, and a wide flange on the drum for finger control during casting and playing a fish. The drum should be wide enough to give a good recovery rate. The Allcock Aerial reel is beautifully made and possesses all these features.

What conclusions can be drawn about spinning reels? Fixed spool reels are versatile enough to cast light or heavy baits with the minimum of effort, but although a large fish can be controlled effectively there will be a certain lack of sensitivity, due to the intervention of the gears and slipping clutch. Multiplier reels are slightly better for playing heavy fish, but less useful when it comes to casting a wide range of weights of lure. You can cast a heavier bait rather further with a multiplier than with a fixed spool, but a good fixed spool will certainly cast a heavy bait quite far enough. I would suggest that the fixed spool is the best choice, because its advantages outweigh its disadvantages to a greater extent than do those of a multiplier reel; but the multiplier is a good second choice, and is very effective in the right hands. The centre pin is the traditionalists' choice and has a limited application. It can be regarded as an obsolescent reel for spinning, though it is still used extensively in other branches of angling.

We have reached a stage when it is possible to marry the rod to the reel. The final choice of rod material must be your own, but it will be found that the points I have raised will be worthy of your consideration. A suitable rod with a level cork handle about sixteen inches long or possibly an inch or two less, depending on the length of your forearm, will be comfortable for single-handed spinning with a fixed spool. The reel fittings should either be sliding rings or one of the newer sliding locking devices. This will allow you to place the reel exactly where you want it. My own choice is about one foot above the rubber knob at the end of the butt. A fixed screw reel fitting is acceptable, of course, if it is well placed, and I would suggest that a rod about eight feet long is a good compromise, giving casting ability without fatigue and reasonable control and hooking power. You may decide, however, that a longer rod is preferable. If this is the case it is likely to be double-handed, and the handle will be about twenty inches long.

It is important to look to the rod rings on spinning rods. They must be of really hard material, as I have already explained, but for use with a fixed spool reel the ring nearest the butt should be very large in diameter, at least three quarters of an inch. Line comes off a fixed spool in a spiral, so check the distance of the first ring from the reel. If it is closer than about twenty inches it

will cut down your casting range. You will find that five rings
are sufficient on an eight foot rod. Typical spacings are, 11
inches, $23\frac{1}{2}$ inches, $37\frac{1}{2}$ inches and $55\frac{1}{2}$ inches measuring from
the tip ring of the rod. These details will vary, of course, from
rod to rod and maker to maker. A seven and a half foot rod,
which I would consider the minimum effective length for a
spinning rod, would only need four rings, and a nine foot rod
would probably need six or seven.

It is worth checking the shape of the cork handle. It should
not flare out like the mouth of a trumpet above the reel, this will
impede the departure of the line because the spirals of line will
strike against it, again less casting range. Sandpaper will cure
this defect!

It is perfectly possible to use a multiplier, or even for that
matter a centre pin reel, with rods furnished as I have just
described, but a rod made specially for use with a multiplier
will certainly have an inset slot with a locking device to hold the
reel and bring the point of departure of the line directly opposite the butt ring. The butt ring may be smaller and much
closer to the reel without disadvantage and a hook for the forefinger is often fitted below the rod (remember the reel is fished
on top so that the thumb controls the running fish?), to give a
better grasp. Ideal rod lengths for casting with a multiplier are
very short, but as I mentioned earlier there is nothing to stop
you using one with a longer rod, or casting double-handed. It is
worth noting that a rod intended for use with a fixed spool or
centre pin reel will serve at a pinch with a multiplier, but the
reverse is not the case.

Lines: the ideal line for use with fixed spool reels is nylon
monofilament. A useful breaking strain for pike spinning is
nine pounds. Heavier line than this may sometimes be necessary
if there are many snags in the water, but the casting performance of the reel will decline. Nylon is rot proof and requires no
maintenance, unlike rods which should be dried after use and
kept well varnished, and reels, that should be dried and oiled
after every outing, but nylon sometimes deteriorates without

apparent cause. It is well worth keeping a reserve supply of new line, and checking the breaking strain of the line in use before you start fishing. I would not advise you to rely on the fish to provide this service!

Multiplier and centre pin reels are better used with braided nylon or braided terylene lines because they lack the springiness of nylon monofilament, which is no great disadvantage on a fixed spool, but can cause trouble on other spinning reels. Braided terylene and hot stretched braided nylon lines lack the stretch of nylon monofilament and this makes them better for striking fish, but unfortunately they do not cast well from fixed spools. Once again no maintenance is required and breaking strains can be rather higher without much loss of casting ability. It goes without saying that it pays to buy good quality line and it is more convenient to wind it onto the reel from spools containing not less than one hundred yards.

Traces: pike have sharp teeth and will bite through fishing lines. For this reason it is advisable to replace the last foot of line before the bait with wire. Perhaps the best wire for the purpose is 'Alasticum', a single strand, blued steel wire that is virtually invisible in the water. It is also flexible without being springy. Someone is bound to say that alasticum wire kinks, but in fact this seldom happens, though when it does the trace must be changed immediately to avoid a sudden breakage. Alasticum wire is obtainable in spools of 50 yards and a wide selection of breaking strains, but I have noted that a greater strain is usually necessary to snap it than that indicated on the spool. The so called 8 lb. wire can be used with confidence in most waters.

Mention has already been made of spinning baits, but the moment has arrived to discuss them in greater detail. Spinning baits fall into two categories, natural and artificial. Natural baits are usually food fish, but there is no ideal choice. Roach, rudd, perch, dace, chub and gudgeon are all good natural baits, but tench and bream are not so good, not because there is any truth in the old story that pike won't eat tench because they are the 'physicians of fishes', there is no truth in either supposition, but solely because they are sombre in colour and less visible in the water, while bream are badly shaped for spinning and casting.

Natural baits must first be caught themselves. It is quite remarkable how these little fish, which suffer from a death wish when you are fishing for tench, barbel or carp in the summer, will eschew the baited hook when you really want to catch them! It suffices to say that the attempt is better made the day before a pike fishing expedition, and that three pound line, a small float, size 16 hooks, and breadpaste or maggots comprise a useful outfit. It sometimes happens that it is quite impossible to obtain a supply of natural baits of species that will be recognizable to the pike as food fish. Do not despair. Sprats, which are obtainable at any fishmongers' shop, are undeniably attractive to pike, indeed there are many anglers who prefer them as natural baits to the freshwater food fish enumerated above. It could just possibly happen, however, that both freshwater baits and sprats are unavailable to the angler. This would not greatly upset the man who prefers the artificial lure, but as I explained in Chapter Four there are many skilled anglers who like to spin with natural baits. Confidence plays an important part in fishing and the angler who has little confidence in his lure will not catch many pike. If you do prefer natural baits, and fresh fish are unobtainable, it is possible to purchase preserved sprats, but they are undoubtedly less attractive to pike on account of the curious chemical smell that emanates from them. A better long term plan is to catch some small food fish (which will be easy because you don't need them urgently!) and preserve them yourself in screw topped jars as a sort of insurance policy, but the formalin should be replaced with a sugar syrup. Fish preserved this way will keep for a month or two, but an even better suggestion still is to wrap them up carefully in paper and place them in the deep freeze of an opulent neighbour. The paper is necessary to disguise the contents of the parcel!

Natural baits can be wobbled, spun or fished sink and draw.

Simplicity is the keynote of all good tackle arrangements and one of the best and oldest wobbling flights is simplicity indeed. A large treble hook is attached to an eighteen inch length of alasticum which is threaded from vent to mouth of the dead food fish. A swivel is attached to the other end of the wire and the line attached to the swivel. The treble hook will pull up

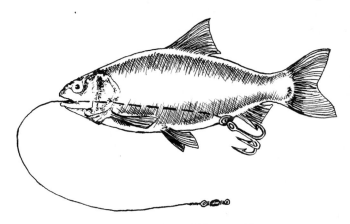

Fig. 4. A simple wobbling tackle.

against the vent of the fish, but to prevent the shank of the hook being pulled into it a shirt button or bead should be interposed. The treble will then remain clear of the bait and be more effective for hooking. Baits attached in this manner will sink, and they can be retrieved at various speeds and made to perform all sorts of pike-attracting wobbles and gyrations, but in weedy, or very shallow water, the bait must be retrieved on, or very near, the surface. A natural bait will only sink very slowly if its swim bladder remains unpunctured, but unfortunately the use of a baiting needle to thread a wire through it invariably does puncture the swim bladder.

An alternative tackle which avoids this difficulty is a treble hooked through the mouth of the bait. Pike, though, cannot be relied upon to seize the bait across its head, and are more likely to seize its middle, so a better hooking device is two treble hooks. One hook is attached to the end of the wire and the second slid down it, so that the distance between them will allow the bait to be hooked through the mouth, and the side or back, about half-way along its length. The wire, of course, should be bound round the shank of the upper hook a few turns, otherwise the weight of the bait will fall on the lower hook during the cast, causing it to adopt a circular or 'au bleu' posture!

The same tackle arrangement is useful for making natural baits spin, but the hook positions shoul┆ be altered so that the lower treble is inserted just in front of the tail of the bait. Shortening the wire between the two trebles will curve the bait slightly, and the distance should be so adjusted that the bait spins when it is drawn through the water. A large bait, however, can be mounted more securely if the wire is taken once or twice round its body, or a third treble is positioned in its flank.

It is often necessary to add weight to such a tackle to make it spin at the right depth, because pike tend to lie low in the water, and experiment will be necessary to suit the conditions, but any weights added should be fastened to the line just above the swivel that joins line and trace. There are a number of

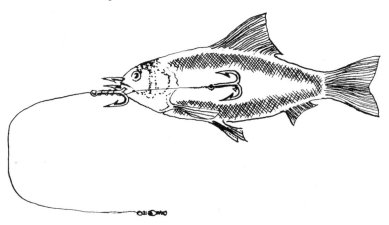

Fig. 5. An alternative wobbling tackle.

different patterns of lead available, and some of them are shaped to give a keel effect to stop the spin of the bait transmitting itself to the line, but if good swivels, which should be as small as possible, are used it is usually unnecessary to employ them. A small bored bullet lead or two or three big split shot will usually do the trick. Bored bullet leads should be stopped above the swivel with two small split shot.

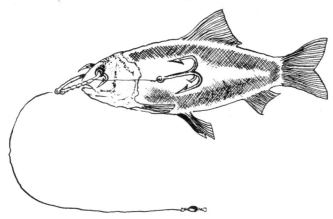

Fig. 6. An improved wobbling tackle (suggested by Fred. J. Taylor).

The novice may wonder why lead should be added a foot, or even rather more, above the bait. The reason is that there is an angle between rod point and the bottom of the lake or river which means that the nose of the bait, whether natural or artificial, is constantly being tilted upwards, and its trim is upset. If a weight is attached, the line is pulling against it and not the nose of the bait, so that the trace between lead and bait will tend to be nearer parallel with the bottom. At the same time leads attached above the bait undoubtedly help it to avoid getting snagged. The amount of lead attached to a spinning flight should be the absolute minimum. Too much lead means a faster retrieve to avoid snagging the bottom, and I repeat that fast moving baits are anathema to big lazy pike!

Natural baits can be fished sink and draw by attaching

trebles to mouth and back or flank, but the weight is attached at, or in, the mouth of the bait, because we want the fish to dive slowly to the bottom, but it is possible to obtain the same effect by attaching the weight above the swivel. I prefer the latter method, because the draw can be started the moment it is felt that the lead has touched bottom, but before the bait, which will follow the lead down, has had a chance to become entangled among the weeds.*

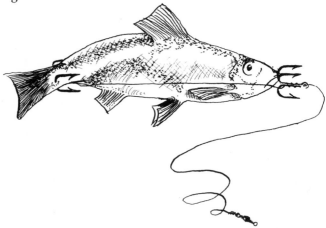

Fig. 7. Basic deadbait spinning flight.

Hook sizes and bait sizes are of interest, but whether you use big or small baits will depend on your feelings about the effectiveness of each. Natural food fish, or sprats five or six inches long, will catch most sizes of pike, while baits of three and twelve inches long would be small and big respectively. A selection of trebles from size 2 down to size 8 will match these baits and should be used in the biggest size that can be attached without looking too obvious.

It sometimes happens that conditions are such that spinning is out of the question, but two-treble hooking tackles can be

---

* Many writers suggest that sink and draw, or trolling tackle, should be so attached that the trace leads away from the tail of the bait, but I see little point in retrieving a deadbait tail-first, and do not recommend this arrangement.

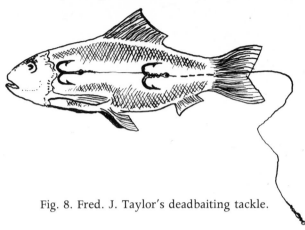

Fig. 8. Fred. J. Taylor's deadbaiting tackle.

used for static deadbaiting, when a larger bait such as a
herring is often employed, and also for livebaiting.

Fred. J. Taylor's rig for deadbaiting is one treble fastened
just behind the gill cover in the side of the bait, and the second
about half-way along its flank. The wire leading from the second
treble is then threaded into the bait and out at its tail. No weight
is necessary. Livebaits are hooked just under the skin in front

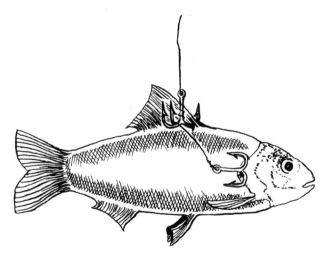

Fig. 9. Livebait snap-tackle.

of the dorsal fin with one treble, while the second is nicked into the bait just behind the gill cover. It will then be suspended from the float in a normal horizontal position, but for legering and paternostering or livebaiting in a powerful current it is often better if the bait is lightly hooked through the upper lip and forward of the dorsal fin, but in such a way that the trebles by the dorsal are the bottom set of hooks, and the trace leads away from the mouth.

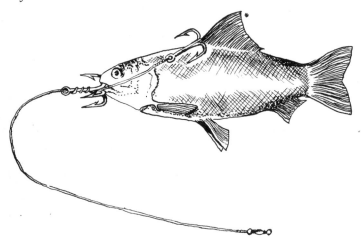

Fig. 10. Livebait snap-tackle for use in powerful currents.

It will occur to most people that livebaiting is a barbarous method of catching pike and that deadbaiting and sink and draw will serve just as well on many of those few occasions when its use is apparently indicated. We anglers could well consider avoiding livebaiting altogether.

The tackle set-ups described in the foregoing paragraphs are not by any means the only ones, but they have all stood the test of time and experience. Many variations will suggest themselves to the angler, and provided they hold his bait in the position or shape needed, and appear to give a good chance of hooking the pike, they will be serving the purpose required of them.

Ready-made flights are available, of course, in the tackle shops. They include designs that incorporate celluloid fins to help induce spin, and lead-covered spikes that can be thrust down the throat of the bait and bent to give it a permanent curve. There are also two- and three-treble traces with sliding hooks, that are useful for livebaiting and deadbaiting, as well as for spinning, wobbling and trolling, but many experienced pikemen prefer to make up their own flights and tackles, so that they can match them to the occasion.

Baiting needle, reel of alasticum, a selection of eyed treble hooks in different sizes, assorted split shot, bored bullet leads and swivels, will all fit into an old tobacco tin. They are the only ingredients necessary for making up virtually every kind of flight or trace you could possibly need in pike fishing—quickly, and on the spot.

Artificial baits, or lures as I prefer to call them, are many and varied but they fall, broadly speaking, into three classes. Those that revolve; those that wobble; and those that dive from the surface to a certain depth, or vice versa. The best known of the revolving lures is the spoon, which is shaped something like the bowl of a spoon without the handle.

The spoon lure in its simple form has a treble hook attached to one end and a ring, or ring and swivel, attached to the other end. It will be seen that such a lure will revolve in its entirety when drawn through the water, but later designs are made so that the top end of the spoon is attached to a stiff wire, that has the treble hook at its further extremity. The blade of such a spoon revolves on, and at an acute angle to, the axle formed by the wire, and is known as a bar spoon. There are literally hundreds of different designs of spoon and bar spoon available, but the best of them have a number of features in common. Firstly, they flash and are visible from a distance. Secondly, they emit a strong vibration. Thirdly, they perform these functions and spin well when they are drawn slowly through the water. The purchase of spoons with these characteristics should be made without forgetting the type of water they will be used in, heavier models will be more suitable for deep powerful rivers than shallow lakes.

It is always advisable to keep a selection of bar spoons in different colour combinations. Most people find that duller colours such as copper, or copper and blue, are better for clear water on bright days, whereas red and silver, or silver, and red and brass, or brass coloured lures, in a larger size, would give greater vibrations and would be more visible in deep and coloured water, or on duller days. The bright metallic colour or dull metallic colour is more important than the red, blue, or what you will, of the secondary colour however, which is there to act as a foil and make the brighter flash more intermittent and interesting. The size of your lure will depend again on your own feelings, but as a general rule it should be smaller for clear water or bright days and bigger for coloured water and dull days. A large spoon would be five inches or so long, and a small one two inches or so.

I don't think there is much doubt that bar spoons possess better pike-attracting qualities than ordinary spoons; they are, of course, a development of them, but an additional advantage is that only the blade revolves, not the bar and hooks, so that little or no twist communicates itself to the trace and line.

A typical modern bar spoon that is readily available is the French Mepps. It possesses all the features mentioned. Sizes four and five are good, and can be cast without additional weights, though weight can be added above the swivel and just above the spinner if necessary. There are, of course, many other good makes of bar spoon available from which a choice can be made, the Mepps is only mentioned as an example.

The wobbling artificial lure always gives me the impression of being something between the spoon and the bar spoon, but it is possible that this is not what the manufacturers intend! They usually look like a twisted or bent piece of metal, or long thin spoon, and are often heavy. When they are drawn through the water they behave in an indecisive fashion, now revolving, now darting off to one side, now climbing towards the surface, now diving down again. They do catch pike, but they do not possess the vibratory element to the same degree as bar spoons. For what it is worth, a friend of mine has fished a variety of waters with both types of lure. He is a skilled and imaginative angler, but the bar spoons bring him more pike, including the specimens of 18 lb. and over. I have a suspicion that a lighter wobbling lure than usual, that vibrated hard as it made its erratic progress through the water would be a real killer!

Wobbling lures, like spoons and bar spoons, come in all colours, shapes and sizes, my own preference nonetheless, is still for bar spoons. I suspect that I echo the view of many anglers more skilled than I.

The third type of spinning lure is usually called a plug. Plugs are an American invention, and I believe they were first developed for use with short baitcaster rods and multiplier reels for bass fishing. They are usually made from wood or plastic and can also be jointed. Typical plugs have a diving vane attached to the nose of their cigar-shaped bodies and float when cast onto the water. When the angler retrieves they dive, wriggling the while.* Some plugs sink, however, and start to wriggle and dive when drawn towards the surface. In doing so they probably emit vibrations. In any event they catch pike but be careful if you add weight because it might upset the action.

The variety of plugs available is enormous. Some of them have adjustable diving vanes, some dispense with them altogether, having a hollow surface on the nose. Other again are long and thin, or short and fat. There are many colour variations. A recent development is plugs made from some rubber-like material that is flexible and does not act as a hook freeing lever in the pike's jaw, but although some good plugs are now being made in Britain the American varieties are usually superior.

It is difficult enough to classify spinning lures, and tackle

* A group of expert pike anglers have been experimenting recently with large surface-working American plugs. They have been very successful when used in places where the weed grows to within a foot or so of the surface.

shops contain many models that combine the functions of more than one type. Some of them are successful, but the novice should try and avoid lures that are designed to catch anglers rather than pike, and if in doubt should look for the features I have mentioned, or take advice from a more experienced angler.

Fig. 11. Typical spring-clip swivel.

All artificial lures can be attached to the line by making a twelve-inch wire trace with a swivel at each end. The swivel nearest the lure should be of the type that has a spring clip or safety clip device, which allows the lure to be easily detached. It is unimportant that the swivels may not have much work to do as anti-kink devices for plugs and bar spoons, because they are a good means of joining line to trace. A loop in the fine wire might well cut nylon line. The bottom swivel can be dispensed with for both bar spoons and plugs if necessary, and a bar spoon sometimes casts better without such a flexible joint at its nose. One last point about all artificials; the body or blade of the lure should not mask the treble hook or hooks.

Expert anglers disagree about the best way to land a beaten fish, but the two usual methods, namely gaff and landing net, are both effective. If you prefer to use a gaff it should have a sharp point, a wide gape and a long handle. The point is inserted under the point of the lower jaw of the fish and I understand that the resulting small hole heals quickly. If a net is used it should be at least two feet in diameter and at least three feet deep. The handle should not be shorter than four foot long, but five or even six foot is better. The nets sold for salmon and carp fishing are suitable; Messrs Efgeeco of Balham, whose products are available at most tackle shops, make an excellent large net. A pair of long nosed pliers and a gag, which is a spring-steel device for holding open the jaws of a fish, are useful for unhooking pike. A spring balance is another necessary item. I suggest that one reading up to 30 lb. is good enough, but optimists may prefer a 40 lb. model!

Playing a pike. A rod held at this angle will apply great pressure. *Photo: Bill Keal.*

Clothes for winter spinning should include a waterproof anorak, thigh waders or wellington boots, and more sleeveless than sleeved pullovers, to allow free movement of the arms. Ordinary gloves are more or less unusable, but leather mittens of the type that shooters use, that leave the fingers free, are good. Woollen mittens attract spinners.

6. Spinning Tactics I: An Outline

TACTICS can be defined as the means employed to defeat an enemy but in pike fishing, as in battles, there are many variables, and descriptions, at this stage, of particular tactics that have defeated pike on certain waters would probably confuse an inexperienced angler, faced with entirely different problems on other waters. I shall, accordingly, devote this chapter to a discussion of the four factors common to every situation in which success is achieved, namely, that we fished in the right place; with the right bait; in the right way; at the right time.

My purpose in so doing will be to show how we can apply our knowledge of pike, and the methods and tackle that are used to catch them, to the tactical problems of spinning, but I have headed Chapters Seven and Eight—Tactics II and III, because the first of them is a sequel to this one, while the second illustrates further many of the points I shall make.

But no discussion of spinning tactics would be complete without reference being made to the preparations that precede their use. I will preface my tactical outline with some observations on this subject.

Tackle should always be checked before leaving home, and the first item to consider is the rod. I suggest that two rods are taken and it is worth checking also that the canvas rod bags do contain spinning rods and not eight foot fly rods! Secondly reels. Again I suggest two. Check that the spools are filled with line to within an eighth of an inch of the rim in the case of fixed spool reels and that multipliers or centre pins, if these are preferred, are reasonably well filled. Test too the strength of the line on the reels to be used, and see that they are well oiled and in working order. Thirdly, check that you have a good selection of artificial lures and plugs in various sizes and colour combinations, and a supply of sprats or other natural baits. (I have not included herrings or livebaits because I am assuming that conditions are known to be suitable for spinning). Fourthly, see that the boxes containing alasticum wire, plain swivels, and swivels with link or snap-on fastener attachments, do actually contain these items, together with bored bullet leads in various sizes, split shot and a selection of treble hooks. Lastly, remember the gaff or net, spring balance, waders or wellingtons, gag and long nosed pliers.

You may wonder why I suggest two rods and two reels. The reason is that it is all too easy to break a rod tip, car doors and boot lids being frequent offenders, while even the best spinning reels are subject to breakdowns at the waterside. I have no doubt that you will include all sorts of items I haven't mentioned but those I have quoted are essential.

It is important to remember ease of movement and mobility in spinning for pike, so it makes sense to lock the spare rod and reel in the boot of the car on arrival at the waterside, and carry all the small items of tackle in old tobacco tins or plastic containers that fit into your pockets, but if you don't own a car it is

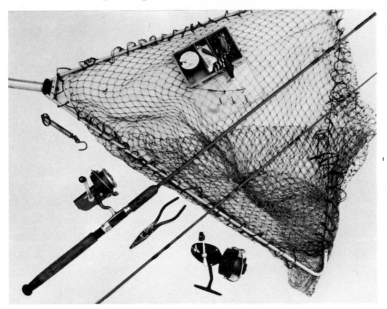

Basic equipment for a day's spinning.

usually not too difficult to find room for a spare reel, and you can chance the necessity for an extra rod. For some time I only owned one spinning rod, and although the action became 'curiouser and curiouser' after the tip had been broken and repaired a few times, it still caught fish! My only fixed spool reel at that time never broke down at all, except on the occasions I forgot to take a spare pick-up spring (the most frequent cause of failure on these reels) and screwdriver with me. In any event travel as light as possible; anglers' umbrellas, camp stools and followers, large tackle boxes and the like are nothing but a nuisance.

Now most of us have probably heard or read that successful anglers spend as much time looking and thinking, as actually fishing. What they are looking for, of course, is suitable swims, and what they are thinking about, is local conditions in order that the right baits can be selected; but pike can see and pike can detect vibrations—reconnaissances should be made without stamping one's feet or appearing unnecessarily visible to the fish.

The factors to be considered in selecting the right place to fish were discussed at some length in an earlier chapter, and I will assume that three or four likely swims will be selected without too much difficulty, but choosing the right bait to fish in the first of them is a problem that becomes more apparent as time passes and no fish are caught!

There are, however, some points that are agreed by most experienced anglers; attention to them and some thought on our part should provide a guide to the sort of bait that might succeed in the conditions we find.

Shallow water suggests light lures or natural baits that don't sink too quickly and foul the bottom when they are retrieved slowly. On bright days in clear water conditions lures should be smaller and duller than during overcast conditions, or when the water is coloured. Pike pick up vibrations—bad visibility due to lack of light, depth, or dirty water suggests a big lure, that vibrates hard and flashes well. Natural baits used in these conditions can be made to flash and also give off vibrations, though not to the same extent as good bar spoons. They do, however, exude a fishy smell.

Weed, if it grows to within a couple of feet or less of the surface, suggests very light lures but a floating plug or surface fished deadbait, i.e. one with an unpunctured swim bladder, might also serve, whereas pockets of weed and deep holes might make us think of fishing a deadbait 'sink and draw'.

Pike will sometimes be seen striking and swirling near the surface. On these occasions floating plugs are a good bet, and so are light lures and natural baits, but heavy lures, or baits that sink fast, would not be such a good choice.

Very cold water makes pike sluggish, but natural baits, twitched along very slowly near the bottom sometimes work in these conditions.

The basic problems of choosing baits and lures for use in

rivers do not differ materially from choosing them for still waters, but it must not be forgotten that the current helps them work or spin. They can thus be retrieved very slowly and still work well. Additionally lures and baits are forced downstream and even towards the surface if they are too light, or insufficiently weighted, which bears thinking about, because the current can also be used to work a bait into just the sort of inaccessible spot that often harbours a 'big un'!

It is not intended, or course, that these points should be accepted as golden rules, but they do help to show how we should think about choosing lures or baits. I hope that it will now be realized why it is that anglers who arrive at the waterside with rods made up and favourite spinners or baits attached catch fewer pike than more experienced men.

I have touched on the right place and the right baits, subjects that will recur in this chapter, but before elaborating on how we might fish the various lures and baits, which is probably the most telling part of tactics in spinning, I must pause in order to explain how the gear is assembled and the cast achieved.

It goes without saying that rod rings must be in line when the rod is put together, and the reel must also be in line with them, and firmly attached. Once the line is threaded through the rings it should be examined to see that it does not go round the rod between any pair of rings; believe me this often happens!

The next stage in the proceedings is to attach a swivel, to stop line kink and act as a union between the line and the wire trace, but if weight is required in the shape of a bored bullet lead it should be slid up the line before the swivel is attached.

A good knot for joining line to swivels is a tucked half-blood knot, and to tie it we must first pass the end of the line through the eye of the swivel. Next, we take the end of the line and pass it round the main line five times and then tuck the end of the line between the main line and the line passed round and round the main line, just where it bends round the eye of the swivel, but without letting it go through the eye. It is as well to tuck the end of the line through, by the swivel, a second time before holding the swivel and the end of the line between finger and thumb of one hand, and pulling on the main line with the other hand to tighten the knot. The knot so formed does not slip when used with nylon, but take care to test it and see that the coils of line around the main line lie snug, and are

Fig. 12. A good knot for tying nylon to swivels: stage 1.

not crossed over each other. The loose end of line should be cut off not less than an eighth of an inch from the knot, which can be quickly undone by digging one's nails into the nearest coil to the eye of the swivel, and pulling away from it.

The next thing to do is to attach a foot length of alasticum wire, if an artificial lure is to be used, or about eighteen inches

Fig. 13. The same knot pulled tight: stage 2.

if it is intended to use a natural bait. The wire is attached to the swivel by passing about an inch of it through the eye and then bending it back so that it lies across the main wire at an angle of forty-five degrees. The two wires can then be twisted firmly round and round each other, to give a sort of plaited effect, but the twist, of course, must be as tight as possible and should be continued until all the shorter length is used up. Do not use pliers to help the process because it is easy to damage a fine trace.

Wire is attached to hooks in exactly the same way as it is to swivels, but when two hooks are to be used, which is usually the case, the upper hook, nearer the swivel, should be attached by passing the wire through the eye of the hook and several

Fig. 14. Attaching Alasticum wire to a swivel: stage 1.

times round its shank, it then continues on its way to be firmly bound to the lower hook. The advantage here is that the upper hook can easily be shifted up or down the wire by undoing the turns of alasticum that lock it in position, and it can thus be adjusted to accommodate any size of deadbait.

The penultimate stage in our preparations is to attach the

Fig. 15. Attaching Alasticum wire to a swivel: stage 2.

deadbait, or bind on a link swivel to which an artificial can be fastened, and artificials can be quickly and easily changed if this type of swivel is employed. Lastly, the bullet lead must be stopped from running up and down the line by placing one split shot above it and another beneath it. The lower one should lie snug against the line-to-swivel knot. Swan shots can be added in the same place, of course, if these suffice as weights.

We have now completed our preparations, but a novice will be unable to fish his bait correctly unless he knows how to reach the fish with it in the first place.

A bait is projected to the right area in lake or river by means of a cast. One of the best descriptions I have read of casting a spinning bait suggested that the caster should try and imagine he was holding a stick, on the end of which was a ball of heavy clay. The motion required to flick such a projectile in any particular direction is not dissimilar to the movement needed to cast a spinner. The main difficulty in casting is the timing of the line release, but don't despair if you don't succeed in an hour or two; an afternoon's practice, preferably with tuition from a competent friend, should enable you to cast with some accuracy, and it helps to start with a fairly heavy bait, an ounce for example. Instructors, however, are not always available and if this should be the case proceed as follows:

Fixed spool reel, single-handed cast, performed with right hand. Open pick-up. Hook forefinger round line, trapping it so that the lure or bait hangs with the first swivel about six inches clear of the top ring. Hold the rod vertically and then drop the tip back slightly, so that the rod is pointing over your shoulder at an angle of about forty-five degrees. Flick the rod sharply forward, and during the time it is passing the vertical open the finger, thus releasing the line. The bait should fly out in the direction required.

The presence of trees and bushes at the waterside sometimes make overhead casts impossible and on these occasions a cast from one's left or right-hand side is useful, but in really cramped conditions a short flick cast can be made from under the rod if the handle is held high, and the tip is pointed towards the water, but there are, of course, may other casting positions which circumstance and your own common-sense will suggest to you.

Casting with a multiplier reel is similar in principle to casting with a fixed spool, but a sharper flick is needed to help the weight of the bait overcome the inertia of the spool and start it

A landing net like this would not be too big for a thirty-pounder.
Photo: Bill Keal.

spinning. At the beginning of the cast the ball of the thumb of the right hand is placed firmly on the drum and is lifted at the critical moment, this movement replaces the finger straightening movement that allows the line to run free from a fixed spool reel. The cast with a multiplier is usually started with the rod pointing back over one's right shoulder but any other position that still allows the thumb to release the drum at the critical moment can be employed.

It is possible that an overrun may occur during the time the bait or lure is flying towards the water, because although the bait is gradually slowing down, the drum of the reel continues to revolve at high speed, thus releasing surplus line. I explained in the last chapter that good modern multipliers have internal braking systems that do much to monitor the speed of the drum and eliminate overruns, but it is as well to remember that one's thumb is useful as a brake, even if it is generally only applied to stop the drum revolving as the bait hits the water, or if it looks like overshooting the target area. Overruns, when they do occur, whether on multiplier or centre pin reels, cause tangles of astonishing proportions; fixed spool reels, of course, cannot overrun, but the forefinger can be used to slow, or stop the line as it leaves the spool.

The double-handed cast, useful with a longer, heavier rod, is made with one's left hand below the reel in the case of a right-handed cast. The lower hand pulls and steadies as the upper, reel controlling, hand pushes—imagine trying to knock an apple off a tree holding a pole with both hands and you will grasp the idea.

Left-handed casts, of course, are the reverse of right-handed casts for all types of reel.

I am quite unqualified to even begin to talk about casting spinners from centre pin reels. Indeed, as a token of my inadequacy, I have given away my Ariel reel, and even refused the gift of a Hardy silex. If you must learn how to perform this minor miracle you should find a good instructor!

Now I started this chapter with a definition of tactics,

because there is an obvious application to spinning for pike. The choice of a military connotation was quite deliberate, however, because I wished to stress another military facet of tactics at this later stage, namely, the importance of putting oneself in the mind of the enemy. I am not suggesting, of course that pike should literally be treated as enemies, but the angler who applies this train of thought, and has some understanding of his quarry, is much more likely to outwit pike than he who chooses to ignore their known characteristics.

We know that pike are lazy fish that generally prefer to lie near the bed of a lake or river, and that their eyes are sited towards the top of their heads. The bait that moves slowly, in the lower part of the water, will cater to these idiosyncrasies. Pike are predatory. The bait that gives an impression of being something out of the ordinary by moving irregularly, or appearing to be crippled, will arouse their interest and their predatory instincts. Reels with a fast retrieve encourage one to retrieve fast and evenly. I see from my records that during one rather successful season's fishing I used a veritable antique among fixed spool reels. To retrieve line at all it was necessary to wind vigorously, which constantly jerked the rod point with the result that my baits travelled slowly in a series of fits and starts. An empirical solution perhaps, but effective! Do remember then to spin low, unless you are fishing over weed in shallow water, or the pike are clearly near the surface, and spin slow, making the lure or bait behave in an enticing manner at all times.

A sensible plan for fishing a suitable area in a river is to start by casting downstream under one's own bank and slowly increase the angle of the casts until one is fishing directly across the stream, but it is sometimes difficult to retrieve a bait slowly that has been cast upstream because it must move faster than the current if it is to work or spin correctly. It is only really feasible to fish upstream in rivers with a gentle flow.

We should not forget that baits need time to sink to their operating depths, and that weights are often necessary to keep them there against the force of the current which will tend to push them downstream and towards the surface.

Heavy artificial lures in rivers are perhaps not so versatile as light lures. Apart from the fact that it helps to be able to vary the weight, the currents tend to push a light lure into a higher plane than the weight on the trace, so that even if the weights touch the bottom the light lure rides clear. Salmon fishermen use buoyant wooden minnows with an uptrace lead to achieve just this effect, but if a heavy lure is felt to be bumping along the bottom it is usually not long before it bumps into a snag! Remember that plugs may not work so well if weight is added

A small pike jumping furiously in its efforts to shed the hooks.
Photo: Bill Keal.

to them. This often limits their use in rivers with a good flow, though they can always be used in the slacks—slacks often hold pike too, and there are, of course, sinking plugs; though they usually lack the specific gravity of weighted lures.

Spun or wobbled natural baits are also best fished deep and slow in rivers under normal conditions, i.e. when fish are not showing near the surface or believed to be in very shallow water, and the problem of weight still applies. There are many occasions too when trolling—fishing sink and draw—is very effective in deep holes under the banks, and in weedbeds close to the bank. Even with a shorter rod the bait can usually be swung out from under the rod point and dropped in the right place, if the distance between tip and first swivel is four feet or so. Sink and draw tactics can also be used over larger areas and greater distances as a variation of the spun or wobbled retrieve, the bait now being cast in the normal way.

Fishing still water is rather different from fishing a river because there is no current and the pike may be lying at a good distance from the shore, but the procedure is not dissimilar; all the water in a likely area should be searched and the same principles apply. Time must be allowed for the lure to sink, and weights, or weight of lure should be kept to a bare minimum, because the only justification for weight in still water is to give casting distance. Distance, of course, is often necessary, but heavy lures are likely to foul the bottom during a long slow retrieve. What's the solution? Natural baits are heavy and fairly buoyant in the water, but they tend to break up with vigorous casting. Plugs are often heavy which helps casting, and a floating plug is not a bad choice for a long cast over shallow water, but even sinking plugs are not the answer to fishing deep, a more usual situation when a longish cast is necessary, because they don't vibrate and flash to the same extent as good bar spoons. Flash and vibration, of course, are useful in conditions of depth and poor visibility.

One suggestion is to move closer to the fish! I often use a rubber dinghy for spinning for pike, but a punt, if available, is much more comfortable. Failing a boat it is worth remembering that even in still water the lighter artificials tend to ride clear of the bottom if preceded by an uptrace weight, but this reminds me that casting a decent distance, i.e. in excess of thirty yards or so, often leads to the spinner flying along behind the weight, which is a more streamlined projectile and thus overtakes it in mid air. The resulting tangle isn't serious but a spinner that has 'kicked back' over itself or the trace doesn't work well when it is retrieved! There are two cures for this trouble. The first and best one is to check the line slightly as the lure nears its destination. The weight being closer to the rod than the lure is first to feel the effect of this slight retardation and the spinner overtakes it, thus hitting the water first and in good order. The second cure is to add a weight just above the spinner which evens matters up, but be careful if you do this that you don't also eliminate the reason for having an uptrace lead in the first place!

There are some waters, large reservoirs for example, which are very deep indeed, thirty feet or more. With a normal cast the lure would be rather close to the angler by the time it had sunk to the operating depth, i.e. near the bottom, so a re-arrangement of the tackle is required, to allow for an exceptionally long cast without 'kick back'. I myself have not fished in these particular circumstances, but an ingenious solution to this problem, suggested by John Nixon in the *Art of Pike and Perch Fishing,* is to place a large bullet lead on the trace, right against the nose of a large vibratory spinner. The position, size and shape of the bullet keeps the lure away from the trace during the very powerful cast, and the resistance of the lure to the water, and the great depth, mean that the lure is tending to be lifted away from the bottom during the long retrieve that follows. I imagine that the lure is worked just fast enough to keep it clear of the bottom.

Plugs come in many shapes and sizes. They can also be sinkers or floaters. A sinking plug can be made to wriggle and dart attractively just above the bottom of a lake provided the

A beaten pike is drawn over the waiting net. *Photo: Bill Keal.*

water isn't so deep that a flashing vibrating spoon would be more effective. My own change-over depth would probably be six or seven feet for a normal sinking plug if the water was clear, and much less in coloured water. Floating plugs have a special application when there is only a foot or two of water above weed, or when a pike is seen basking in a hole in the weed, because they can be made to dither and wriggle on the surface in a most attractive manner, they can sometimes be used on rivers too in these conditions. Floating plugs that dive too steeply are not the ones to use in these circumstances, they dive into the weed at the slightest provocation, but deep diving floaters which usually dive to about five feet or so can be used in just the same way as sinking plugs, provided the water is not so deep that the plug is working too close to the surface to be effective in non-surface working conditions.

Spinning techniques for natural baits in still water follow the same pattern as those in rivers, but there is no current to help work the bait, which means that the angler must concentrate all the more on retrieving it in a pike-attracting manner. Weights can usually be kept to a minimum or avoided altogether.

It is impossible to predict precisely the right time to fish for pike because they are capricious feeders, and their feasts are definitely of the movable variety, but I think it is not unreasonable to suggest that the angler stands a chance of catching fish at any time of the day during good conditions, because the majority of the pike in the water are likely to feed at some time. Conversely, fewer are likely to do so in poor conditions. The anglers' chances of coming across a feeding fish will diminish accordingly. Nonetheless, there are very few occasions indeed when there isn't a pike somewhere in the water that is prepared to be tempted by a skilfully presented bait or lure. The only problem, of course, is finding such a fish!

The remarks above apply to pike fishing in general, but they also have considerable bearing on two reasons why spinning techniques will often succeed when other methods fail. They in their turn are particularly significant when the right time to fish is considered, so I will not be departing from the point if I mention them now.

The angler who chooses to spin for pike is not defeated if he fails to hook one, even though he has fished two or three suitable lures or baits with skill and intelligence in a likely area; he just moves to another suitable spot and tries again, modifying his tackle and technique accordingly. His chances of eventually catching a fish are still immeasurably greater than those of the live or deadbaiter, because he covers many more fish than they, and has more techniques at his disposal.

The second reason is that the spinner, unlike the live or deadbaiter, is not even dependent on finding feeding fish, because skilfully worked spinning lures will often take fish that aren't feeding at all and would refuse a live or dead bait, so there is always a chance for the spinner if conditions allow spinning;

there are very few occasions when this is not the case. And even on waters that appear equally suitable for either spinning, live or deadbaiting, the spinner should still catch more fish, again because more will be covered by spinning techniques than either of the other two methods.

Many anglers place great reliance on certain times of day being better for pike fishing than others, and there is little doubt that there are optimum periods during both good and bad conditions. These optimum periods sometimes, but not always, occur sufficiently often at the same time of day on any

Unhooking a pike: the gag is used to keep its jaws apart. *Photo: Bill Keal.*

particular water for a pattern to be established, but it won't necessarily apply on another water; for this reason I will not suggest that early morning, or the last hour before dusk, for example, are better for pike fishing than any other period, but it does make sense to be ready to fish in a good area at any time that experience of the water in question suggests is likely to be an optimum period. In the absence of such experience, or on any day when an expected pattern fails to establish itself, the angler should still be alert, firstly because the pike may come on feed at any moment, and secondly because a real monster may be on the prowl—which could be why the smaller pike are not in evidence!

I will summarize the subject of the right time to fish by saying that the really determined angler, whose morale remains high despite adverse conditions and who fishes hard and intelligently for as long as possible, whenever possible, will frequently have several weighty reasons for knowing he fished at the right time, whereas the man who stays at home will certainly catch nothing at all.

It will now be clear, I hope, that the four factors essential to success in all conditions, and on all waters, are worthy of our consideration. We should, therefore, constantly ask ourselves four questions, 'am I fishing in the right place? with the right bait? in the right way? at the right time?'. By so doing we will not only remind ourselves of the points we should always consider, but will also ensure that we apply the full scope of our knowledge and intelligence to the tactical problems of the moment.

7. Spinning Tactics II: Hooking, Playing and Landing Pike

I BELIEVE those stories of mighty pike that smash rods and snap lines; of ashen-faced anglers trembling at the strength and fury of monsters hooked and lost; of giant fish whose jaws are festooned with broken tackle, legends in their lifetime. But I also believe that there would be fewer of these tales, if more anglers understood the special problems of hooking, playing and landing fish as large and powerful as pike.

Pike will not be properly hooked unless the strike is made at the right moment and with sufficient force to drive the hooks into their bony jaws.

The right moment to strike, when spinning with an artificial bait, is as soon as it is realized that a pike has seized the bait, and a pike normally takes with sufficient élan to make it abundantly clear that it has done so: but there are also times when the take is almost imperceptible, perhaps because the pike had been following the bait and was actually overtaking it as it seized it. On these occasions the inexperienced angler usually believes that his bait has touched the bottom, or brushed past a weed, and he fails to strike. The pike, however, realizes his mistake immediately and hastily ejects the bait.

There are times too when the progress of the bait is arrested with heart-stopping suddenness; the angler quite correctly strikes, but on feeling no movement he concludes that the bait is snagged. Then, just as he lowers his rod to avoid straining it, and pulls hard on the line to free the bait, the 'snag' surges powerfully away, snapping the taut line in the process.

I believe that a big pike, and in my own and other people's experience a pike that fails to react immediately to a powerful strike usually is a big one, behaves this way because it does not realize it has been hooked, but whatever the reason, the fact remains that there can be something very fishy about snagged baits; they should be treated with circumspection!

Pike can usually be struck instantly when natural baits are used for spinning. It must be remembered, however, that they won't necessarily eject the bait if the strike is delayed, but will move off, turn and swallow them in just the same way as they would any other food fish; provided, of course, that their suspicions are not aroused by ultra-heavy tackle, or the reek of preservative. Nonetheless, I would still recommend an immediate strike, in order to ensure that the fish is hooked in the jaws and not far back in its throat. The only exceptions I would make are if very large baits are being used or the take is half-hearted, in which cases a few seconds can be allowed to pass so that the pike may grasp the bait firmly within its jaws.

It is by no means unusual for an inexperienced angler to completely forget to strike, particularly if the take is violent, which is often the case. I suspect that excitement gets the better of him as the rod whips over, the reel screams and it is evident that a fish is 'on'. The pike may, of course, be adequately hooked, but all too often the hooks are only lightly lodged in its jaws and an unexpected manoeuvre on the part of angler or pike is all that is necessary to dislodge them, so do remember that pike must always be struck unless the bait has been gorged —if this is the case the angler had no right to be fishing for pike in the first place.

Most anglers use the adjustable, two-treble, Jardine snap tackle that was described in an earlier chapter for livebaiting and usually strike when the movements of the line or float indicate that the pike has turned the bait and moved off on its second run, but the Jardine snap tackle was actually designed to hook the pike if the strike was made during the first run. Once again my own preference is for an early strike unless a very large bait is being used, but it is worth remembering that those indefinite movements of the float or line which suggest that a fish is only toying with the bait could also be caused by a large pike that has engulfed it on the spot and has no intention of moving off to turn it in the usual manner. The start of the second run, however, is a good time to strike when fishing a static deadbait in cold weather, and I imagine that the pike, being sluggish in the very cold water, are in no hurry to swallow the large baits usually employed; which would explain why most fish caught by using this technique are correctly hooked in the jaws.

The moment to strike when fishing any technique in which natural baits are used will, of course, depend to a considerable extent on the tackle and bait and how they are deployed, the way the pike takes the bait, its size relative to the bait, and the judgement and experience of the angler concerned. The whole subject in fact is open to many personal interpretations and it is not surprising that the opinions of the experts are at variance. My own preference, as you will have gathered, is for an early strike if possible. I believe that it is more sporting to be reasonably sure of hooking a sporting adversary in the mouth, which means that it can be returned to the water undamaged to grow bigger and fight again, than to hook it in its throat or

Another pike falls for a spinner. *Photo: Angling Photo Service.*

stomach—the eventual consequence of allowing too much time before making the strike.

The strike itself can be made in much the same way whether we are spinning, livebaiting or deadbaiting, but the line must always be taut between rod point and bait just prior to the strike, or some of its force will be wasted. In spinning, of course, the line is always fairly taut, but the live or deadbaiter will reel in any slack and 'feel' the fish before he strikes.

The position of the rod at the start of the strike is important. It is best held low and parallel to the water, with the line at right angles to it. This ensures that a long strike can be made, and the greatest amount of leverage applied. An angler who retrieves his bait with the rod pointing skywards must not only lower it before he can strike effectively but may also give slack line for a moment in doing so. A moment is all a pike needs to eject an artificial bait! Both these difficulties will be overcome, of course, if the bait is retrieved with the rod held low in the first place.

I believe that the best way to make the strike is to bring the rod back in a long powerful heave. My own procedure, which has served me well, is to strike to one side rather than vertically, because the upper jaw of a pike is even more impenetrable than the rest of its physiognomy, and a vertical strike tends to pull the hooks upwards. Towards the end of the strike I remove my forefinger from the spool of the reel, where it had been placed to stop line being given during the strike, and shift my left hand to the handle of the reel. I then wind furiously to seize the initiative at the start of the fight and to bring the rod forward to an angle of sixty degrees or so with the water.

It is, in my opinion, unnecessary to repeat the strike just described unless the bait was taken when it was more than say twenty-five yards from the angler, in which case its effectiveness could be nullified by the elasticity of the line, but I cannot subscribe to the view, held by some anglers, that pike should always be struck several times; firstly because the hookhold could actually be loosened by so doing and secondly because there is a danger that slack line will be given when the rod is lowered between strikes.

The 'how' like the 'when' of striking has always been a much disputed point among the experts, but John Bickerdyke's comments on the subject in *The Book of the All-Round Angler* are as applicable today as they were in 1888, the year the book was first published, so here they are:

'The Strike—There are great differences of opinion among our best pike fishermen as to how a pike should be struck. Mr Pennell says strike, and go on striking until, by the kicking of the pike, it is clear the hooks are into him. Mr Jardine says do not strike, but give a long, steady pull, and hold the pike hard for a few seconds, to get the hooks well home. My own opinion is that no rule can be laid down which can be applied to all, or even the majority of cases. When the tackle is fifty yards or more from the angler, Mr Pennell's hard strike, possibly repeated, is necessary to overcome the elasticity of so much line, and to lift it off the water. The same strike, when the tackle is five yards from the angler, would assuredly break the line. Then, again, if the bait and consequently the triangles, are large or plentiful, a heavier strike is necessary than when they are small or few. I can only say one thing for certain—that great judgement is necessary, and that it is particularly in the strike that the novice can be distinguished from the practised angler. The roof of a pike's mouth is bony and affords bad anchorage for a hook; but the tongue and lower jaw are good holding ground; the strike should, therefore, be rather sideways than up. Always be sure that you do not strike on a slack line. First gather in a little line, until you can all but feel the pike, and then strike at once. A harder strike should be made with a pliant rod than a stiff one, and with a short rod than a long one.'

Playing a pike is a very different kettle of fish, if you will pardon the expression, to playing a salmon because it is unusual for a pike to make very long runs or leap from the water, but although the melodrama may be absent, the brute strength and stubbornness are certainly present. A big pike will often fight for just as long, or even longer, than a salmon of the same weight hooked on similar tackle.

A good way to weigh a pike. *Photo: Bill Keal.*

The first point to remember when playing a pike is that a rod which is held so that the butt is at right angles to the line, which in practice means at an angle of about sixty degrees with the water, will not only exert the maximum pressure of which it is capable but will also act as an excellent shock absorber. A rod that is pointed towards the fish being played, however, can serve no purpose whatsoever, while a rod that is held so that it points backwards over the angler's shoulder will take all the strain on its upper joint; exert less pressure on the fish; and possibly break into the bargain.

The second point to note is that although it may be impossible to actually stop a big pike that is running towards a snag or obstacle of some kind, it is usually possible to make it change direction by applying sidestrain. The way to apply sidestrain is to lower the rod until it is parallel with the water and use it as a lever to pull the pike's head round, so that it continues to run—but away from the obstacle. Once again the rod is held so that the line and the butt of the rod are as near as possible at right angles to each other.

The object of subjecting a pike to constant pressure is to tire it as quickly as possible, but from time to time it will be necessary to give or retrieve line, while still maintaining pressure. My third point, therefore, is concerned with the way the reel is handled in conjunction with the rod.

Centre-pin and multiplier reels are ideal for playing pike because a running fish can be controlled by braking the drum of the reel with one's finger or thumb. In addition both types of reel usually possess ratchet or drag brakes, which help to maintain pressure and obviate overruns should control be lost for an instant at the start of a run. Retrieving line with either centre-pin or multiplier is simply a matter of winding with the rod held in the right position, but contact with the fish is so direct and sensitive that it is easy to judge when line must be given again and also how much pressure to apply to the drum of the reel.

Playing a fish when using a rod that is fitted with a fixed spool reel is by no means difficult or complicated provided that the slipping clutch is set correctly, and its use understood.

A suitable adjustment is made to the clutch by tightening the control capstan until the clutch just begins to slip as the rod bends towards the point when butt and line are at right angles to each other. Thus, when a fish makes a sudden run the rod will whip over, but the clutch will give enough line to avert disaster at just the right moment.

Unfortunately, however, more pressure is needed to make the clutch slip in the first place than is needed to keep it slipping and the rod will quickly begin to straighten, and the strain on the fish will be lessened, unless the resistance offered by the clutch is augmented by finger pressure on the lip of the spool. This means, effectively, that the spool can be braked in just the same way as the drum of a centre-pin or multiplier reel is braked to apply sidestrain or otherwise allow a fish to run against a controlled and directing resistance.

The technique used to retrieve line, when playing a heavy fish on a fixed spool reel, is called pumping the fish. It is effected by winding against the strain so that the rod is literally wound down towards the fish, whereupon the spool is locked by finger pressure and the rod lifted to draw the fish towards the angler. Its use is necessary because an attempt to bring in a heavy fish by winding in the normal way would only set the clutch slipping, and to wind against a fish while the clutch slips destroys our control and kinks the line. Pumping will not be necessary, of course, to bring in smaller fish or large fish that are so tired that they are unable to pull hard enough to start the clutch slipping, and in these instances line can be retrieved just as if we were using an ordinary centre-pin reel.

The points I have made so far are mainly concerned with the correct use of our equipment, but it will be to our advantage to have some knowledge of a pike's reaction to being hooked, and the tactics it will subsequently employ to avoid the indignity of capture. Forewarned is forearmed!

A pike's reaction to the angler's strike is either to rush off; allow itself to be wound unprotestingly towards the angler; or appear to ignore the incident by giving the impression that it is a snag.

The first reaction mentioned, that of rushing away, is the most usual and it will be countered by applying enough strain

A nineteen-pounder from the upper Lough Erne. *Photo: Angling Photo Service.*

to turn the fish from any snags or weedbeds that are visible, but the second and third reactions are occasioned, I believe, because the pike does not actually realize that it has been hooked.

Now I described at the beginning of this chapter the action to be taken, or rather the action not to be taken, when a fish appears to be a snag; such a fish, having been well struck, will eventually move off on a conventional first run and can be dealt with accordingly, but a pike that is wound to within yards of the bank will become extremely angry and frightened when it first catches sight of the angler, and realizes that all is not well.

A frightened, angry pike on a short line will do more than make those short powerful runs with sudden changes of direction and borings towards the bottom that are the most typical characteristics of a pike's struggle for freedom; it may jump right out of the water; jigger, the term used to describe a fish that appears on the surface and shakes its head furiously in an effort to dislodge the hooks; or make a long, savagely powerful run in an attempt to reach a weedbed or snag.

Jumping and jiggering, are best countered, not by giving slack line, but by lowering the rod and trying to draw the fish back under the surface, and a powerful run will be countered by sidestrain, followed by steady pressure if we succeed in diverting the fish towards open water, but a point that is worth remembering is that sidestrain can often be increased if we move along the bank until we are better placed *vis-à-vis* the fish.

Fishing from a boat presents another problem because the fish may run under it and foul the anchor rope. The answer here is to always anchor the boat at one end only, when it should be possible to pass the rod round the free end of the boat while still maintaining enough pressure to keep the pike clear of the rope; the battle can then be resumed on the other side.

Yet another tactic that pike employ with success is to pretend to give up the struggle. They lie sullenly on the surface and the angler relaxes and reaches for the net. Then just as success is within his grasp. Bang! The pike tears away again. The bang, of course, is the line breaking!

I will conclude my remarks on playing pike by saying that a good pike must not be allowed to run wherever it likes under too light a pressure, nor must it be subjected to too heavy a pressure except in cases of dire necessity.

The reasons for not letting a fish do exactly what it likes are obvious, but the reasons why it can be disastrous to hold good fish too hard are, firstly, that the hooks may be literally torn from their jaws and secondly, because pike have a disconcerting habit of suddenly changing the direction of their runs. This means that the rod is often called upon to absorb an unexpected extra pressure, because a split second elapses before line can be given, whatever type of reel is used. A rod that is already strained to the limit is unable to absorb a further shock and could well snap in these circumstances, but even if the rod withstands the strain, the line is unlikely to follow suit!

The newcomer to pike-fishing may well be daunted by the foregoing paragraphs: he should take heart. The most lively and exciting fight is usually that given by a pike of fifteen pounds or so, and he is likely to gain plenty of experience with fish of this calibre before he hooks a really big pike. A really big pike, though it will probably fight for longer, and will make very powerful runs, is unlikely to be so fast, which will give him more time to anticipate its next move!

The final act in the drama is to land our fish, but it is important to be absolutely sure that a pike is completely played out before any attempt is made to do so. That last plunge against a high held rod and short line has shattered the hopes of many an angler!

We can insure against the consequences of a last plunge by slackening the clutch a turn. The next step is to draw the fish gently over the net which should be held still and submerged in the water, or towards the gaff, if this is preferred, which should also be held ready in position. The fish can then be lifted out in one easy movement.

Some last points. Last minute plunges are often provoked by poking at the fish with net or gaff, and there is also a real danger of getting the hooks caught in the net while the fish is still outside it, in which case it will often wrench itself free. Equally, an inexpertly handled gaff will sometimes break the line.

Hooking, playing and landing pike successfully is a matter of experience and common sense, but it is possible to learn quite a lot about the right things to do (and for that matter the wrong things!) by hearing and reading about the experiences of other anglers. For this reason I am firmly of the opinion that all fishing books should contain àt least one account of the capture, or even loss, of an exceptionally big fish.

The story I shall tell you concerns a big pike. It began on a weekday, when I read my horoscope in a morning paper. 'Tomorrow', it said, 'will be a great day for those with an interest in sport.' Intrigued, I bought an evening paper. 'You will realize a sporting ambition tomorrow' it predicted.

It is clearly a great mistake to tempt the fates by trying to change one's destiny: a visit to the office on the morrow would have been quite unthinkable!

I awoke early the next morning with the realization that I was far too ill to go to work, but at nine o'clock I forced myself to get up, and a little later, purely for the sake of my health, I ventured forth to do a little fishing.

Ten o'clock found me treating my condition in a rubber dinghy which was afloat on the grey waters of a small lake. By lunchtime I had caught nothing and was seriously considering changing both my morning and evening papers.

By mid-afternoon I was desperate. To add to my difficulties a strong wind was blowing and the dinghy was drifting, in spite of a brick tied to the drogue rope. Every hour or so I had to retrieve both brick and drogue, getting sopping wet in the process, head for the shore, and stagger back to the other end of

A study in concentration: Spinning on Lough Ree. *Photo: Bill Keal.*

the lake in order to fish down it again. I was nearly blown off my feet several times while carrying the inflated dinghy and kept dropping bits of my equipment.

At about 3.30 p.m. I drifted into a little bay at the leeward end of the lake. The water here was shallow, not more than three feet, but I remembered that Fred. J. Taylor had told me that big pike were sometimes to be found in the shallows. I decided to fish the bay for a last half hour, before giving the pike best and going home to a hot bath. Whilst I had been thinking about the problems of fishing the bay, however, the dinghy had been creeping towards the shore, which was now no more than twenty yards away. To stop it drifting any further I anchored it, by tying my gaff to the drogue rope. This, as we shall see, was a mistake!

My next mistake was to assemble an old carp rod and cast a herring, suspended two feet under a big float, to bob attractively on the waves twenty yards or so to my right. I was tired and fed up by this time and it seemed an admirably lazy way of continuing to fish while I smoked a much needed cigarette. Eventually, having finished my cigarette, I picked up the spinning rod and armed it with a number four copper Mepps bar spoon.

At the second cast I hooked a weed. The third cast fell in the same area and again I hooked weed, but just as the spinner freed itself it was seized by what I could have sworn was a rather small pike, which allowed itself to be wound to within two yards of the dinghy.

Then it happened. The water boiled and erupted beside me. An absolutely enormous pike appeared on the surface, so close I could have leant over and touched it.

In the corner of its mouth was my copper bar spoon.

I remembered immediately that I had failed to strike hard, so convinced had I been that only a small pike had taken the bait, but just as my forefinger dropped to the spool of my Altex reel the pike saw me. The water boiled again as it surged away. The rod bent through a greater number of angles than I would have believed possible. I refused to give line for the second needed to drive home the hooks, but although I distinctly felt the trace wire thrum across the pike's teeth, both line and rod stood the strain.

With trembling fingers I slackened the adjuster on the slipping clutch—this was a fish I mustn't lose!

The pike ran for twenty yards or so, towards the open water, then it turned abruptly and headed straight for my deadbait float! I applied sidestrain until I was sure that something must give. The fish turned with a tremendous swirl not a yard from the float.

Twice more in the next quarter of an hour tragedy was narrowly averted, but finally, after a long succession of short but tremendously powerful runs, the huge fish surfaced and lay supine five yards away from me. The fight was over. With my left hand I groped for the gaff. The gaff! Of course, it was hooked round a lily root at the bottom of the lake!

My heart fell; all I had to land the fish with was a small net, fourteen inches in diameter. It was quite big enough for fish of four or five pounds—but this fish!

Still, there was nothing for it. Sick with apprehension I drew the monster alongside and slid the net over its head. This was the moment I dreaded. I was sure it would make a last plunge, and that would be that! In fact it tried to do so, but by this time half of its enormous length was in the net which was fortunately fairly deep. I dropped the rod and wrapping my right arm round its body and heaving with the net I dragged it into the dinghy, shipping gallons of water as I did so.

Paddling shorewards, sitting on the fish, I realized that I would have to leave it alive and unattended for a moment while I climbed out of the dinghy. I was worried it would jump back into the water. Fortunately, some men who had been watching the fight were waiting on the bank and fish, dinghy and a damp, exhausted, but deliriously happy angler were dragged ashore together.

The rule of the water was that all pike must be killed and

this was done, but I was extremely anxious to know the weight of the fish. All I could tell was that it weighed more than the magical thirty pounds, the limit of my spring balance. The thought crossed my mind that I might just have pipped the English record which then stood at $37\frac{1}{2}$ lbs.

It was not to be. The correct weight, as ascertained at a railway station two hours later, was exactly 33 lbs. The length of the fish was 3 ft. $10\frac{1}{2}$ ins., the breaking strain of the line was $9\frac{1}{2}$ lbs., that of the trace, 8 lbs.

8. Spinning Tactics III:
Interesting Days on Various Waters

THE VILLAGE I live in stands beside a small river which that absorbing book, *Where to Fish,* describes as follows: 'Excellent coarse fishing; lower reaches noted for chub, bream and tench; trout higher up.'

Where to Fish is amazingly accurate; indeed it once provided me with the name of a Welsh hill-stream so insignificant that even its owner didn't know it had one, and it was right too about the trout it contained, but I sometimes wonder if the trout attributed to our river are only included as a well-meant sop to local sensibilities—I have yet to see, far less catch one in the four miles of water that lie between my home and the source.

As for the pike and other fish that inhabit the extreme upper reaches, the 'finny denizens' as a friend of mine insists on calling them, well, theirs is an uneasy existence; the river runs clear and shallow between high muddy banks in winter, is clogged with lilies in summer and ravaged by floods in autumn. The fishing, however, can still be good, witness the eighteen-pound pike that was caught by a friend's young brother, and there is always the chance of a two-pound perch or a large tench.

I made my first visit to the river one summer, but as soon as I saw the water I realized that my selection of plugs and spoons would be useless—the surface was almost entirely covered with lilies, and the largest pool I could see was less than four feet in diameter.

I wish I could say that I had anticipated the situation; of course I hadn't; this meant that I had to return home, find and make up some float tackle, and devote the rest of the morning to catching small rudd in a local pond.

I returned to the river after lunch. I had little experience of trolling in really weedy conditions in those days and it took me a little while to learn the trick of so releasing the line that the deadbait dropped neatly and quietly through the holes in the lilies. I learnt too that it was pointless to cast any distance because the bait would be pulled into the weed on the draw instead of being lifted out without touching it.

Eventually, having lost most of my small rudd, I decided to concentrate entirely on the holes under my own bank, and it wasn't long before a lean shape flashed out from under the lilies and seized the bait.

During the next half-hour I caught two more pike, both rather larger than the first, and a fine job I had landing them, what with the heavy weed-growth and high bank, but my eight pound line was no match for the next chap I hooked, which was a pity, he took the last of my baits and felt like a real 'good 'un!'

The secret of successful trolling, of course, is to work the bait so that it looks like a wounded fish that is struggling feebly towards the surface and then sinking to the bottom again. I would suggest though, that you use a longer, more powerful rod and stronger line if you mean to use this method much in summer because such an outfit makes it easier to fish the distant pools and bully hooked pike over the weeds before they have a chance to dive under them. I would also advise you to stick to small baits—an instantaneous strike is an absolute necessity in heavily weeded waters, and it is far more likely to connect if the pike can engulf the bait.

As it happens I have not fished our river much in summer since the occasion I have just described; there are too many ponds in the district holding tempting stocks of sizeable tench and carp; but a description of a well remembered winter's day will illustrate a point I wish to emphasise, namely, that pike can be the most unpredictable of creatures.

The first thing I noticed when I arrived at the waterside that frosty January morning was that the river was very low and clear. It had too, a cold, greenish look that boded ill for my chances. But didn't the Reverend Tom Seccombe-Gray hook his thirty-pound Wye pike in a pool that was fringed with ice?— He did, and the account he gives of the capture of that fish, in *Pike Fishing, Red Letter Days and Others* now, alas, out of print, must surely rank as one of the most exciting descriptions ever written about a battle with a monster pike.

But to return to my own experiences. It is well established that a natural bait, worked slowly or not at all, is usually the best choice when the water is bitterly cold. For this reason I started fishing with a small sprat, casting it into all those places that could possibly provide concealment for a pike and inching it slowly back along the bottom. In this fashion I fished about a mile of river—without moving a pike. Eventually I found myself on a high bank that overlooked a bend where there was a deeper pool. Quite suddenly I had a feeling, not only that the pool contained a pike, but also that I should catch it.

The novice may well be surprised, or even amused, that I should have entertained such thoughts on a day when I had already spent several hours fishing without the slightest sign of success; but older hands will know that these feelings are by no means uncommon in angling: they know too that their instincts seldom betray them.

I cast the deadbait to the head of the pool. Twelve casts later I was still fishless. Perhaps I wasn't an old enough hand or the cold had blunted my instincts! On the thirteenth cast (I'm sure it was the thirteenth!), I lost my bait and half the trace.

I pulled another sprat from my anorak pocket and was amazed to find that it was lovingly entwined with an Allcocks floating plug.

A plug in the hand, however old, battered, and rusty in the hooks, is an easier bait to attach to half a wire trace than a sprat and its attendant trebles; without more ado I threaded the last inch of the wire through its nose ring, bent it back and twisted it tight. Then I cast out again to the head of the pool.

The old plug behaved in the most erratic and uncontrollable fashion; they usually do if they've seen much use, or the loop in the wire, or the eye of the swivel, is insufficiently large to let them work freely, but the very first time it did dive properly —bang!

That pike fought well considering the cold, indeed there were one or two moments when it seemed to be doing rather better than I was. In due course I managed to land it—one of my better fish from the river.

A couple of casts later, using the same plug, I caught another fish, probably its mate. I walked back to the car in high good humour.

Now these were not the sort of fish the leader writers laud in the angling press. Nevertheless they, or rather the events which lead to their capture, serve to make my point: pike are unpredictable. And if the method that our own and other people's experience tells us is most likely to succeed fails to work for once, why, we should ring the changes—rather sooner and with greater intelligence and application than I did!

Oh, I nearly forgot to tell you. Seccombe-Gray caught that thirty-pounder on a small artificial lure.

This business of not being hidebound reminds me of another

trip I once made, this time to Sussex. My intention was to fish a lake of six or seven acres that lies below a large country house.

The pool had been formed by damming a small stream, and it is typical of the country house lakes that we now accept as being an integral part of the countryside. But how many of the anglers who fish these waters today are aware that they often owe the peace, tranquillity and pastoral beauty of their surroundings, not in the first instance, to nature herself, but to the efforts of Kent, Capability Brown and the other great landscape gardeners of the eighteenth century? Perhaps Brown himself was an angler; certainly he loved making lakes; and his very first commission was to design one for the Duke of Grafton.

Taking scales for scientific examination. Fish scales yield much information about age and growth rate. *Photo: Bill Keal.*

On the Saturday morning my own peace and tranquillity was shattered by a telephone call from London. A friend, an enthusiastic angler, who at that time had no experience of pike fishing, wished to join me on the Sunday.

Now this friend is one of two particular angling companions of mine who seldom read fishing books, invariably fish with unsuitable tackle and just as invariably catch fish. They are in fact born anglers. Knowing this I should have been warned!

We drove to the lake after lunch. 'The best area', I said, 'is that little bay; there's a deeper hole in the middle of it and on a cold day like this that's where we'll find the pike'.

My companion nodded, unimpressed, and helped himself to one of my cigarettes.

'The best way to fish the bay', said I, 'is to drop your spinner beyond it and work it back through it.'

I did so. My spinner, a Mepps No. 4, landed exactly where I had pointed. I retrieved it slowly, jerking the rod point and occasionally changing the direction of its travel. The pike and my companion remained unmoved by the artistry of my performance.

I made perhaps two dozen casts. Nothing happened. I moved to the next bay, a larger one, and repeated the performance. Still nothing happened. I tried a third with the same result.

'Doesn't look as if the pike are going to feed this afternoon; temperature's dropping', I remarked.

I must confess I was baffled and annoyed. The last time I had fished there had been at the beginning of a thaw, but half the lake had still been covered with ice. I and two other members of the local angling club had caught nearly a dozen fish in less than an hour. We had all used vibratory spinners.

By this time my companion had assembled his tackle. His spinning rod, if I may so describe it without offending the manufacturers of real spinning rods, was an extraordinary mixture of World War I tank aerials, whalebone, and binder twine. His fixed spool reel had the dejected air of a french aristocrat after the revolution. The last time it had been oiled

was before it left the factory. His line was Japanese gut substitute. My younger readers will not remember this substance.
They need not perturb themselves.

Courteously, I offered him one of my well-tried Mepps
spinners. Equally courteously he refused it. From the bottom of
his gangrenous fishing bag he produced a lure of his own. It was
bright orange, much articulated, and of curious design. If I had
been a pike it would have terrified me out of my wits! Eschew-
ing such niceties as swivels and wire traces he knotted it with
many grannies to the end of his line. He then pirouetted
clumsily around for a minute or two and hurled it towards the
middle of the lake. It landed just five yards from the bank. He
wound in. The rod bent. Three minutes later he landed a
goodish pike.

In ten casts he caught four more. Then he detached the orange
horror from his line and handed it to me. 'Here', he said, 'try
this, perhaps you'll do a little bit better!'

I will never forget the lesson I learnt that day. Now, when
I go spinning, I carry a wider variety of baits and lures. I don't
start blaming the pike or the weather for my lack of success
until I've given all of them a trial.

It's odd though, I've never caught a pike on the orange
horror!

An old school-friend of mine has stocked a small river with
trout. One day he asked me to help him remove the few pike
that had somehow survived the Water Board's recent electric
fishing purge.

We started fishing in a tiny weirpool. P.E.W's first cast,
which landed beneath the lasher, produced a beautiful brown
trout of about three pounds. Sheepishly, he returned it to the
water. My own cast found the slack water beside the fall. A
moment later I had a pike on the bank. As you may imagine I
was greatly relieved that it wasn't I that caught that trout!

We were unable to tempt any more fish from the weirpool,
though it did contain another pike that followed my lure to
within feet of the bank. Then it saw me and sheared away. We

Fred. J. Taylor caught this pike on a trout-rod. Bait? a lure-fly!
Photo: F. J. Taylor.

decided to come back later.

Half a mile upstream we, or rather P.E.W., who has eyes like a hawk, spotted another pike. It saw us at the same moment and dashed downstream. All caution forgotten we raced after it.

We chased that pike from one retreat to another for about ten minutes. Finally it came to rest and lay panting between two furrows of golden sand. The water was eighteen inches deep and crystal clear.

Purposefully, P.E.W. unhooked the spinner from the butt-ring of his rod. I stared at him in amazement.

'You haven't a chance—it's seen us and it's scared stiff', I said.

I don't remember the details of the wager we made, but I do remember being confident that I would win it.

Several minutes passed. P.E.W. continued to cast and retrieve, the pike continued to ignore the lure. On the thirtieth cast, or maybe it was the one hundred and thirtieth, the pike surged forward and slashed furiously at the bait. A minute later it lay kicking in the brambles. The treble hook was still firmly embedded in its upper jaw.

A few months later I caught a pike from my father-in-law's stretch of river in Berkshire.* With my next cast I hooked another pike. It felt heavier and fought more strongly than the first fish but as soon as I had it ashore I saw that it was exactly the same size. I bent down to unhook the spinner. Lo and behold, it was the fish I had returned to the water less than five minutes earlier! The marks of the hooks were clearly visible.

I have told you about P.E.W's trout-stream pike and my Berkshire fish because I want to comment on the unusual circumstances of their capture. I am sure, you see, that both of them were frightened. Yet the majority of anglers believe, as I had hitherto believed, that a frightened fish won't feed.

Is it possible that these fish seized our lures because some other emotion, anger for instance, overrode their fear? I don't

* Marrying the daughter of a man who owns some fishing is a brilliant tactic. My bachelor readers should note it well.

suppose we shall ever know; but I think it is significant that salmon, which have hardly ever been known to feed on their way to the redds, will frequently accept lures *after* they have been offered to them dozens of times. Could it be that they do so in sudden anger, as we swat flies? Nobody knows—yet. But there could be a connection, and I for one will not be surprised if anglers in the future use lures that are actually designed to irritate or otherwise influence pike into taking them.

We anglers are well served by two lively and well-informed newspapers and a number of first class magazines. Yet there are still some people who refuse to believe that 'book learning' has any part to play in angling. They point with pride to old Bloggs. 'Never read a book in his life', they say, 'just look at the fish he brings home.' Bloggs may well catch fish: but is there an angler alive whose ability is so great that he has nothing to learn from the varied experiences of other anglers? I don't think so.

I sincerely believe, however, that if all the Bloggses were to read about fishing for just a few minutes every week, they would not only broaden the scope of their angling activities and catch more and bigger fish, they would also derive a keener pleasure from their sport. Nor need they despair when times are unseasonable or old age makes fishing but a cherished memory. There waits for them a wealth of angling literature.

Let me now give you one example of how the written word made me think again about an aspect of piking and show how it led me to an excellent morning's fishing.

The gist of the article in the angling magazine (unfortunately its author's name escapes me) was that pike might feel inclined to feed at first light. They would, after all, been unable to do so during the night, and in winter the night is very long.

To a non-angler this would seem a rather obvious suggestion, but it would probably be rejected out of hand by many dyed-in-the-wool pike men, raised in the tradition that winter fishing is a waste of time until after a late-ish breakfast. I read the article and dismissed the thought from my mind.

Fred. J. Taylor with four nice pike. The clip devices are American stringers: they are used to keep the fish alive in the water after capture. Pike secured in this fashion will probably suffer far less damage than if they are kept in a keep-net. The fish shown here were all safely returned to the water after this picture was taken. *Photo: F. J. Taylor.*

Months later I was travelling on a train that was much delayed. In the bottom of my briefcase I found the magazine. I re-read the article. The more I thought about it, the more it made sense.

I launched my rubber dinghy in total darkness the following Sunday morning, and paddled it stealthily into a favourite bay half-way round a small lake. The dawn, far from being rosy-fingered, was heralded only by a steady paling of the sky. With a sense of relief I started fishing.

The lure I selected was an old vibro spoon. It was taken on the first cast within feet of the dinghy. Seven pounds, a good start. I fished on. A quarter of an hour later I had another fish, two pounds, again as the bait neared the boat.

I have no doubt that my reader will have deduced by now what I had so far failed to notice—the fish were hunting near the surface. It needed a violent swirl and a glimpse of a broad spotted flank to bring the point home to me.

Swiftly I changed my lure for a floating plug. Fishing a plug on the surface in these conditions is the greatest fun. You give the reel a couple of turns—the plug dives sharply. Pop! There it is again. A sideways pull. It skitters and skids. I often find that the pike take it when it is motionless, but I'm sure we shouldn't leave it still for long enough to give them time to think about it. Attract them with a sudden movement, give them a second to grab it. Grab it they did too. Six more fish in twenty minutes' frantic fishing. Then quiet. The fish had gone deeper. A quick change back to the bar spoon brought four more fish, but the intervals between them were longer. The best fish of the morning was twelve pounds.

It was broad daylight by this time. An old man, walking by the lake, stopped and stared at me in amazement. 'Hey!', he shouted. 'You won't catch much at this time of day!'

I repeated the experiment a fortnight later. Conditions were perfect. It was warmer and there was a gentle breeze from the south west—I caught my first fish at tea time. That's fishing for you!

In fact the morning was by no means uneventful. To begin with I foulhooked a tench. How that fish fought! Somehow the spinner had caught it in the side. At five and a half pounds it was far bigger than any tench I'd ever caught by design!

The next occurrence was the sudden appearance, not ten yards from the boat, of a dorsal fin so large that I could hardly believe my eyes. It cut through the ripples in a gentle half-circle. Then it sank from view.

I have seen the dorsal fins of two pike weighing more than twenty-five pounds: they were dwarfed by this one. Assuredly its owner was a pike that would have broken every record in the book.

Sick with excitement I cast towards it. The line promptly caught in the pick-up. I unhooked it and cast again. And again. During the next half hour I tried to tempt that fish with two varieties of lure in various sizes, several plugs, a sprat and finally a herring. It was casting that herring that put the permanent bend in my split-cane spinning rod.

Leviathan is still there. Tomorrow, the first day of a new pike season, I shall try for him again.

9. 'Other Business'

THE CAPTOR of a really big pike will be faced with two major problems if he decides to have it 'glass-cased'. Firstly he must find a taxidermist; secondly, the fee.

Taxidermists are few and far between these days and you will only have about forty-eight hours to find one even if you catch your monster in winter. After that nature will begin to take her course and she won't make any secret of it! A taxidermist that I can recommend, having seen numerous examples of his work, and having made something of a study of the subject, is Mr E. N. Hare of 60 Hamilton Road, London N.W.11. Mr Hare is more than a skilled craftsman, he is an artist. (He is also an enthusiastic angler). As for the fee, I believe that the cost of setting up a really big pike is in the region of forty to fifty pounds, but you will have to wait at least four months for the work to be completed—plenty of time to start saving!

One thing I don't advise is 'do-it-yourself' taxidermy. I first tried it after reading Colin Willock's book *Coarse Fishing*. I still have the greatest respect for Mr Willock, whose books and articles I enjoy, but taxidermy is not, in my opinion, as simple as he suggests. Even my best effort looks as though it has been savaged by a crocodile!

But you may prefer to return your giant fish to the water, yet still wish to keep a permanent record of it. In this case the answer is a photograph. I am no photographer but it would seem sensible to take at least half a dozen shots of the subject, showing it in different positions and varying the exposure. At least one of the resulting pictures is bound to be a good one and this can be enlarged to full-plate size or even larger. The fish will show to greater advantage, of course, if its captor is slightly built!

Record books too are useful for noting your catches, but do use one that allows enough room for plenty of details to be inserted; it is surprising how helpful they can be. I have learnt, for example, that I have never caught a decent tench from one particular local pond before 7 a.m., in spite of having started fishing at dawn on many occasions. No more early rising for me! Equally, there is invariably a blank period in the middle of the afternoon on a pike lake I know, whatever the conditions. I can see this by studying my records of the three seasons I have fished there.

The best way to kill a pike, incidentally, is to hit it hard with a heavy blunt instrument just where the top of its head meets its body, but mention of killing pike inevitably raises the question of whether we are morally justified in doing so.

My own views on this controversial issue are quite clear in my mind. I have no quarrel with anglers who occasionally kill 6 or 7 lb. fish for the table, or really notable fish because they wish to have them set up. Nor do I disagree with the policy of killing pike in trout streams or any other water where their presence is obviously undesirable. I do, however, take great

Ken Taylor, one of the famous Taylor brothers, unhooks the plug from the jaws of a pike. *Photo: F. J. Taylor.*

exception to those selfish individuals who kill all the pike they catch for no reason whatsoever. Such behaviour may not have done any great harm to our pike stocks a hundred years ago when anglers were few. It is inexcusable today when there are probably more than a million pike-fishermen, most of whom are more mobile, more leisured, and better equipped than their Victorian forebears.

I take exception, too, to the use of keep-nets in pike fishing. Either the fish is to be killed or it is to be allowed its freedom. If it is intended to free a pike it seems rather pointless to first confine it for several hours in a keep-net. It will lose much of its protective slime and probably damage its fins.

Moral considerations apart, the pike and other fish probably have less to fear from anglers than from water pollution and abstraction. The battle against pollution is slowly being won, due to a growing public awareness of the problem and the efforts of the Anglers Co-operative Association, an organisation to which we should all subscribe, but abstraction is still increasing and will continue to do so until it is realized that conservation, not abstraction, is the answer. By that time it will be probably too late.

Now for three items I should have mentioned in earlier chapters.

The first of these is that well-known ruiner of top-joints and tempers, the snagged bait. The *wrong* way to set about freeing a snagged bait is to heave on the rod until it looks like a hairpin. You will not be applying maximum pressure to the bait because the rod will absorb much of the strain—too much! The right way to apply as much direct pressure as possible is to lower the rod tip until it is pointing towards the snag. Then pull on the line as hard as you can, without actually breaking it. The

Morning at Knipton Reservoir, where the second largest English pike was caught. *Photo: Angling Photo Service.*

chances are that the bait will free itself. If it doesn't, try to obtain a pull on it from the opposite direction. Still unsuccessful? Then you must 'pull for a break'.

A word of warning. Before you start hand-lining apply a steady pressure with the rod for at least a minute to make absolutely sure that the snag isn't a big pike!

The second item is the snagged fish. Again hand-lining is often effective. But be careful! A big pike that is suddenly freed from the encumbering weeds or rotten tree-stumps is not interested in the painful fact that the line is still wrapped round your fist! An alternative course of action, should hand-lining fail, is to slacken off the pressure entirely in the hope that the pike will swim clear of its own accord. Both these tricks work . . . sometimes. Perhaps the best solution is to stop the fish reaching a snag in the first place!

The third item is the hooks we use. Many pike are lost after being played for quite some time because the hooks were blunt and did not penetrate properly in the first place. Hooks must be kept razor-sharp and if the barb is too protuberant, which is frequently the case, it must be reduced. Both these operations can be performed satisfactorily with the aid of a small, fine cut file.

Finally, some thoughts about the waters that hold those elusive big pike.

A glance at any long list of specimen pike reveals that more really big fish are caught from still or nearly still waters than from rivers and an outstanding example of a big pike locality in England is the Norfolk Broads, which recently produced a forty-pounder; but there are two rivers, the Herefordshire Wye and the Hampshire Avon, which have always produced their quota of 30 lb. plus fish and each of them in its time has also yielded an English record.

The three waters mentioned are very different in character but one thing they have in common is that they are all noted for the high average size of the other fish they hold. A further point that is common to each of the rivers is that both of them have a run of salmon and sea-trout as well as holding brown trout and large coarse fish.

A further glance at the specimen lists shows that the great lochs of Scotland and loughs of Ireland, which are of course larger than the majority of our English waters, produce bigger pike too; while Lomond and Conn, which as you will remember produced the Scots and Irish records, are not alone among them in having runs of salmon and sea-trout in addition to thriving populations of brown trout and coarse fish.

The inferences I draw from this information are as follows: first, that a really extensive lake is a likely home for a really big pike; second, that sheer size of water on its own is insufficient, there must be a plentiful supply of large food fish, third, that a good supply of large food fish is a very important factor in producing pike up to about 40 lbs. It is significant, I think, that there is a boosted supply of large food fish, in the shape of a salmon and sea-trout run, in both of the only two English rivers that consistently yield pike in excess of 30 lbs., and the Norfolk Broads, of course, are famous for their vast shoals of sizeable bream and rudd.

In contrast, the lists also show that it is exceedingly rare for really big English pike, i.e. fish in the thirty-pound plus range, to be caught from very small rivers or lakes of less than about eight acres; but it is not that unusual, relatively speaking, for one of the smaller waters to produce the odd fish of 25 lbs. or so.

Most of us, of course, do not have the good fortune to live within easy reach of famous big-pike waters, but *Where to Fish,* an ordnance survey map, the angling grape-vine and a little knowledge of some of the factors that encourage pike-growth will certainly help us to pinpoint likely local waters. If these include lakes, gravel pits, reservoirs, canals or rivers holding decent fish of other species, particularly bream, rudd or roach, then the chances are that the pike, too, will reach a goodish size.

I think you will find that spinning is an enjoyable method of fishing for pike:—I am certain it is the most successful.

BIBLIOGRAPHY

BARRETT, W. H. *A Fisherman's Methods and Memories*. Seeley, Service & Co. Ltd. London, 1953.

'B.B.' *The Fisherman's Bedside Book*. Eyre & Spottiswoode (Publishers) Ltd. London, 1945.

BICKERDYKE, J. *The Book of the All-round Angler*. L. Upcot Gill. London, 1888.

BRENNAND, G. *The Fisherman's Handbook*. Ward Lock & Co. Ltd. London, 1951.

BUCKNALL, G. *Big Pike*. E.M. Art & Publishing Ltd. Peterborough, 1965.

Fishing Days. Frederick Muller Ltd. London, 1966.

CHOLMONDLEY-PENNELL, H. *Fishing, Pike and Coarse Fish* ('Badminton Library'). Longmans, Green & Co. Ltd. London, 1885.

The Book of the Pike. R. Hardwicke. London, 1865.

FORBES, D. C. *Catch a Big Fish*. George Newnes Ltd. London, 1967.

GAMMON, C. *Hook, Line and Spinner*. William Heinemann Ltd. London, 1959.

HAMPTON, J. F. *Hampton on Pike Fishing*. W. & R. Chambers Ltd. London, 1947.

HOWES, W. J. *Spinning for Coarse, Sea and Game Fish*. W. Foulsham & Co. Ltd. London, 1962.

JARDINE, A. *Fishing*. 'Country Life Library of Sport'. George Newnes Ltd. London, 1904.

MARLBOROUGH, D. *Fishing in Ponds*. Herbert Jenkins Ltd. London, 1966.

MARTIN, J. W. *Days among the Pike and Perch*. W. Brendon & Son Ltd. Plymouth, 1907.

MARSHALL-HARDY, J. *Angling Ways*. Herbert Jenkins Ltd. London, 1934.

NATHAN, W. *Gone Fishing*. William Heinemann Ltd. London, 1960.

NIXON, J. *The Art of Pike and Perch Fishing*. Oliver & Boyd Ltd. London, 1964.

PARKER, L. A. *This Fishing*. Cleaver-Hume Press Ltd. London, 1948.

SECCOMBE-GRAY, T. *Pike Fishing*. Heath, Cranton Ltd. London, 1923.

SENIOR, W: et al. *Pike and Perch*. Longmans, Green & Co. Ltd. London, 1900.

SPENCE, E. F. *The Pike Fisher*. A. & C. Black Ltd. London, 1928.

TAYLOR, F. J. *Angling in Earnest*. MacGibbon & Kee Ltd. 2nd ed. London, 1967.

Various authorities. *Fine Angling for Coarse Fish*. Seeley, Service & Co. Ltd. London, 1947.

WALKER, R. *Still-Water Angling*. MacGibbon & Kee Ltd. 3rd ed. London, 1960.

WALTON, IZAAK. *The Compleat Angler or Contemplative Man's Recreation*. London, 1653.

WARD, A. L. *Pike: How to Catch Them*. Herbert Jenkins Ltd. London, 1954.

WETHERALL, N. L. *Pike Fishing*. H. F. & G. Witherby Ltd. London, 1961.

WIGGIN, M. *Troubled Waters*. Hutchinson & Co. (Publishers) Ltd. London, 1960.

WILLOCK, C. *Coarse Fishing*. Faber & Faber Ltd. London, 1955.

The Angler's Encyclopaedia. Odhams Press Ltd. London, 1960.

INDEX